# Supernatural

By
Keith Allan Shields

© Copyright 2020 Keith Allan Shields

No portion of this book may be reproduced in whole or in part, by any means whatsoever, except for passages excerpted for the purposes of review, without the prior written permission of the publisher.

For information, or to order additional copies, please contact:

Beacon Publishing Group
P.O. Box 41573 Charleston, S.C. 29423
800.817.8480 | beaconpublishinggroup.com

Publisher's catalog available by request.

ISBN-13: 978-1-949472-13-4

ISBN-10: 1-949472-13-4

Published in 2020. New York, NY 10001.

First Edition. Printed in the USA.

All rights reserved.

Table of Contents

Introduction: An Author's Confession

Chapter 1: Breakfast with an Atheist...9

Chapter 2: A Thought Experiment...24

Chapter 3: Why Me, Lord?...36

Chapter 4: A Theology of Miracles...48

Chapter 5: A Few Good Miracles...65

Chapter 6: Good News to Celts...83

Chapter 7: On Science and the Supernatural...95

Chapter 8: Describing Supernatural Experiences...107

Chapter 9: Birth of the Pentecostal Movement and the Purpose of Signs...114

Chapter 10: Walking in the Dark...126

Chapter 11: When Miracles Don't Happen...141

Chapter 12: Why Do We Long for Something More?...152

Chapter 13: How Shall We Then Live?...161

Works Cited

## Endorsements for *Supernatural*

Supernatural is a humble, honest and gentle invitation to see God at work around us. Within hours of finishing the book I had recommended it to a friend and thought of others who would gain from this good read.
*- Alan Jones, D. Min, Lead Pastor of Grande Prairie Church of Christ.*

Just a few days ago the most recent survey about Canadian spirituality concluded that a majority are now in the atheist and no religion category. In the midst of this growing population Keith seeks to add his missional voice as a pastor, musician, scientist, and believer in the supernatural. Without denying the challenges nor the reality of the supernatural he with clarity and authenticity lays out the strengths and issues of being a firm believer in the contemporary power of the risen Christ. Grounded in Scripture, history and personal experience he woos the reader to think deeper. I recommend this as a gift to the seeking friend and for the thoughtful believer as both will benefit from this great read.
*– John F. Caplin, M.A., Executive and Leadership Coach, Church Consultant, and PAOC Pastor.*

Keith wades into the challenging and confusing waters of the supernatural with authenticity rooted in theological reflection and personal experience. He shares his struggle, his search, and his findings and invites honest explorers on a journey of discovery. Supernatural is a must-read for anyone willing to go deeper into the mysteries of how God works.
- *Cam Taylor, author of Between Pastors and Detour*

In his brilliant book, *Supernatural*, Keith Shields grapples with evident encounters of supernatural phenomenon against the practical workings of cause and effect, the empirical systems so familiar to the disciplines of science, to provide a faithful interpretation of the data as he observes God break into time and space. In doing so, Keith challenges the comfortable theological boxes we have created to contain our belief in Empiricism, demonstrating the confidence we can have in God's continuing work. His "humble apologetic" I gladly endorse and pledge to mimic in my own relationships.
- *Dennis Bachman, Lead Pastor/Director of ViaCordis and ViaCordis.online, California*

I've been friends with Keith for many years and have always appreciated the diligence and clarity of his thought processes. In Supernatural Keith brings this same approach to his personal experience and pursuit to understand the miraculous and what that says about faith in or disbelief in God. Keith's honesty and appreciation of those who may not share his same convictions amplify the sincerity with which he writes without diminishing his own convictions. It is a thought provoking and interesting read for all who ponder the possibility of the Supernatural.

*- David Hockley, Minister, Coldstream Christian Church, Greater Vernon, British Columbia*

## Introduction: An Author's Confession

Writing a book and asking others to read it is a daunting task. It can seem rather overconfident to think that what I have to say will be worthy reading material for others. Authors are well-aware of the deficiencies of their work and they know that their books will not please everyone. Some will find the present book to be overly spiritual, sort of "so heavenly-minded that it is no earthly good." Some might say it is too logical and insufficiently guided by the Spirit of God. One reader will find that there are too many examples of miraculous events while another will say that there are not enough examples of the supernatural to carry the main point of the book. Some will find the explanations of some events insufficient to make the claim of "miraculous." Others might find that I have related miracles too far removed from my own life to be of objective value. Writing a book is as much about education and grappling with concepts as it is about providing something from which others might learn. Anne Lamott has said:

> I still encourage anyone who feels at all compelled to write to do so. I just try to warn people who hope to get published that publication is not all it is cracked up to be. But writing is. Writing has so much to give, so much to teach, so many surprises. That thing you had to force yourself to do---the actual act of writing-

--turns out to be the best part. It's like discovering that while you thought you needed the tea ceremony for the caffeine, what you really needed was the tea ceremony. The act of writing turns out to be its own reward.[1]

This book represents some of my own wrestling and consolidation on the topic of the supernatural. It is an exercise in self-discovery that I hope may also be valuable to others.

**Our majority culture too readily ignores the supernatural and seeks only to measure the world with five senses.** Thus, for my part, there is a desire for the events of this book to be given a fair hearing at face value. Yet I am well-aware that each person who opens this book arrives with her or his own perspective on the universe, miracles, science, philosophy, religion, and faith. Let me be the first to admit that this also applies to me, the author. I too come to the topics discussed with my own bias and a perspective that will be unique to the experiences of my life and the ways I have interpreted those experiences. The book is necessarily tied to my own experiences and so I hope that the reader will forgive the autobiographical nature of the book. All of us must give

---

[1] Lamott, A. (2017, April). *TED: Ideas Worth Spreading.* Retrieved June 30, 2019 from
https://www.ted.com/talks/anne_lamott_12_truths_i_learned_from_life_and_writing?language=en

an interpretation of the things we see, hear, taste, touch, and smell. There is no such thing as a pure, uninterpreted event. Nor can we keep from affecting events around us as we seek to interpret our world. The lenses through which we look will affect our sight, and our interaction with the world does have an effect on our environment. If I step close to a thermometer to find the temperature of the room, my own body temperature has an effect on the thermometer. In the same way, our spiritual temperature may also affect the supernatural world and the miracles we see.

Allow me to pause for a moment and address the question, "for whom is the book written?" Of course, anyone can read the book and find value in the reading, but there are some who are highly unlikely to even pick up the book. If you are already settled in your mind that there is nothing in the universe beyond what our five senses can detect. If you believe that naturalistic science has all of the answers to all of the questions of the world (even if we have not yet found all of the answers), then this book is not for you and I would suggest you may want to put it down. It might actually make you angry and that is certainly not a goal of mine. I do not believe that it is possible for this book to take you from one who sees all of the answers necessary in science to one who believes in the presence of God. Furthermore, you may in fact struggle to understand some of my experiences and arguments that are anchored firmly in a Christian framework and parts of the book may indeed be nonsense to you.

So, if the book is not for the natural scientists I have just described, it must have a different audience. We live in a time when a great many people have de-converted from a once-strong Christian faith. Recently, several well-known Christian writers have disclosed that they no longer consider themselves Christians and have left their ancient faith. I will not address the reasons why this is happening on a regular basis at this time in history. Other authors are tackling this question and it could well be the topic of an entire book.[2] I do not know if people such as that will read this book, but I do think if they were to pick it up and give it an open-minded reading it might give them a reason to reconsider the choice they have made. Coming from a previous stance of Christian faith, they would not be troubled by the illustrations and arguments of the book. They may say they have heard it all before, but I would hope that the documented miracle stories might be helpful to their journey.

---

[2] McKnight, Scot, "Recent Stories of Leaving the Faith," Jesus Creed, 2019-08-20;
https://www.patheos.com/blogs/jesuscreed/2019/08/20/recent-stories-of-leaving-the-faith/?utm_medium=webpush&utm_source=evangelical&utm_campaign=JesusCreed

Another potential reader is the one who keeps hearing about those who have left the faith and is bothered by the stories. They hear the testimonies of people like Josh Harris or Marty Sampson who have left the faith and may be convinced to consider doing the same. This book may be just the book they need to stem their serious doubt and allow them to look for the supernatural in new ways. I am especially praying for readers such as this.

Then there are those readers who are solidly in the Christian faith but live like functional atheists or, perhaps at best, deists. They believe in God the Father, ascribe to a traditional sense of the person of Jesus, and the Holy Spirit and believe in prayer, but they haven't seen much of the supernatural in a long time. This book may help to explain why they have not seen many answers to prayer and may encourage them to look for the supernatural within their natural world.

Perhaps lastly, although with more thought I might come up with other types of readers, there is one more type of reader who may be helped by this book. That is the reader who comes across to others as if they have never gone a day in their lives without seeing four or five miracles in the day. These people are particularly annoying to a naturalistic scientist because they see everything as supernatural and nothing as natural. They are the kind of people who gush to others and say, "Did you see that sunrise this morning? Wasn't that a miracle?" To which the naturalistic scientist wants to say, "No, that was just the earth rotating on its axis such that we got to see the sun at the horizon as it shone at a sharp angle through the atmosphere of the earth." I pray that these overly enthusiastic readers might consider their words and be just a bit more considerate of the perspective of others who see things differently than they see them.

Perhaps I am straying too much into the argument of this book. This introduction is meant to explain why this book has been written and encourage the reader to read the rest of it. If I say too much more about what type of reader you may be, I may cause you to get discouraged and stop reading. Suffice it to say that, I encourage you to approach the book with an open mind and I hope that you might find this book helpful, wherever you might place yourself on a spiritual scale. I trust that every reader can learn from reading the book and pray that each will test what it says. **I am one who has always appreciated the logic and mystery of both the scientific world and the theological world. I believe that if we focus on one to the exclusion of the other, we will lack a complete understanding of the universe.** Thus, I write to the scientifically minded person who has little time for the supernatural on any topic of discussion. I write to the person who has little time for anything except what God says in the Bible. I ask that person to consider that God has indeed communicated with the world in more ways than just the Bible. The heavens declare the glory of God (Psalm 19; Romans 1) and the motion of the planets tells us something of the nature of our God. I am hopeful that *Supernatural* will allow you to more accurately hear from and test the words and actions of the Holy Spirit.

A number of people have helped with the writing of this book. Friends and family have been pressed upon to read chapters that appeared suddenly and without warning in their email inbox. Others offered their editorial services to read chapters or the entire work and I have gladly taken them up on their generous offers. Still others offered to help, but due to time constraints were not able to give me their advice on the book. Yet those friends changed the texture of the book because I thought of their perspectives as I wrote portions intended for them to read. Many conversations with those who share my Christian worldview, and many with whom I do not, made my words clearer and more accurate. Editors, both professional and voluntary, shaped the content and structure of this book. I thank you all.

A partial list of those who contributed to this work, either through conversations with me or reading chapters and making comments, includes the following people (italics indicate that I have changed the names to protect their privacy). *Walter*; Bart Campolo; *Robert*; Ryan Scruggs; Jordan Blasetti; Bethany, Twila, and Lauren (my three daughters); *Jason*; *James*; *Adam* and *Linda*; Jamie Hunka; James Watson; Richard Dahlstrom; John Van Sloten; *Martin* and his wife; John Caplin; Bob Logan; the staff and elders of Bow Valley Christian Church; numerous pastors and leaders within churches; atheist friends and agnostic friends.

Tara Miller was the professional editor on this work. Her effort caught many of my mistakes and made the book more readable. The people at my publishing house who worked on the fine details of getting the right format for the book were most helpful. I am indebted to Dr. Anthony Campolo, whose words of encouragement challenged me to write more, write better, and believe in the project. My wife Maureen worked long hours to catch many typos and murky wording. I appreciate her help, encouragement, challenge, and love.

## Chapter 1: Breakfast with an Atheist

I spent an evening and a morning with Bart Campolo and bought him breakfast. Well, 400 others and I spent the evening with him, and 15 others and I bought him breakfast at a Denny's in Calgary. At breakfast, I contributed $50 to a gift for his time spent with me and a group of atheists, de-converted Christians, ex-pastors, a home-schooling mother, and myself: a theologically-conservative, grace-giving, resurrection-proclaiming, supernatural-believing Christian. I am still not sure why I gave $50 to the free-will offering for this conversation. Perhaps I wanted to prove to a group of atheists and secular humanists that a still-believing Christian pastor could be generous. The whole group must have been generous because Bart went home with over $600 after it had been converted to American dollars. The night before, most of the people in the breakfast crowd had also attended a polite conversation (formerly known as a Christian and Humanist debate) at Foothills Alliance Church where Christians, Humanists, Atheists, Agnostics, Back-Sliders, Fundamentalists, and Apologists gathered. The Apologists were there to hone their skills in debating the godless Humanists. The Atheists were there to hone their skills in debating the fundy, hypocritical Christians. Bart Campolo is a former evangelist, former director of a Christian social-justice agency, and famous son of his famous father, Anthony Campolo. Tony Campolo, as he is usually introduced, had been a powerful influence on my life in my early Bible College days. He preached the kind of sermons my fellow pastors-in-training and I aspired to preach and the kinds of sermons we listened to over and over again. I had memorized most of one regarding the American work-ethic and can still quote pieces of it. Bart was the debater, or polite conversationalist, who would represent all of the sons of famous fathers who had left the church, left the faith, and become Humanists.

On the other side of the stage sat our protagonist in this story, Sean McDowell. Here was the other famous son of a famous father, who represented the great hope of the Christian Apologists. Sean is an intelligent, pleasant young man who had just rewritten the definitive textbook on Christian Apologetics with his famous father, Josh McDowell. The book, *Evidence That Demands A Verdict*, now in its "eleventh-first" edition, was also a big hit with me and my mates at Bible College. The point-form style of this book was perfect for quotes in the papers we would write with all the certitude of teenagers who had been given the keys to unlock the mysteries of God, Jesus, and the Holy Spirit. Our professors had more than prepared us to take on any theological argument, and Josh McDowell was just there to back us up. At least that is how it feels when you are 19. In the battle that ensued at Foothills Alliance Church, Sean played the Prophet, the person who continued to call the crowd back to faith, even as the Humanist attempted to poke holes in the arguments put forward for God. Everyone came with *an opinion*, and everyone left with *the same opinion*. **As the Beatles said in their song *Eleanor Rigby*, "no one was saved."** But then again, no one lost their faith that night, unless they had already lost it before they came to the event. After all, it was a polite conversation in a polite Canadian church.

One thing was quite clear that night: Bart Campolo is a force to be reckoned with. Tony Campolo is known for his convincing rhetoric and charm. Bart is equally as charismatic as his father. His monologues and mini-sermons were captivating, both in front of the general audience at the church and at breakfast the following morning. He is a leader who commands attention and entices people to follow him. He is also sincere in his disbelief in God and winsome in character. His present mission is to create small group fellowships all over the world where people live in community seeking to be the best atheistic, secular humanists possible.

Bart made it quite clear that the reason he was no longer a Christian was that "he could no longer believe in any of the supernatural religions." He told us that by the time he totally lost his faith, it had been a "death by a thousand cuts." He slowly lost sight of the supernatural and answered prayer, and his faith dwindled. To quote an

Eagles song, "there was no final scene, no frozen frame,"[3] he just watched his faith slowly fade away.

Bart Campolo is not alone. Many today are slowly losing their faith; or have already lost their faith and have not yet realized it; or have a weak version of a Christian faith. A significant component in this loss is that many have lost a supernatural understanding of the universe and have ceased to see signs, wonders, miracles, and other aspects of the supernatural. As the Western world has discovered and explained more and more through science, as the Christian-bubble of protection for the faith has slowly eroded, the religious person has awoken in a world of science and sometimes forgets that God is behind the science. Things that once would have been attributed to the powerful work of an unseen God are now most likely attributed to the work of science and medicine. Some of this is might be rightly attributed to medicine, while some is not. Those who believe in God must certainly recognize that it is God who invented science and medicine. **How does one realistically distinguish between acts of God and acts of medicine?** The lines are often blurred. I must say again for emphasis that all of our medicine and science can be attributed to the supernatural God who created a world in which humans are capable of discovering the nature of biology, physics, chemistry, and mathematics.

---

[3] "Waiting in the Weeds," Recorded by The Eagles, on the *Long Road Out of Eden* album, 2007, songwriters: Don Henley / Steuart Smith.

Contemporary genetics including such recent developments as CRISPR genetic manipulation can trace their history back to people like Gregor Mendel and Francis Collins, many of whom had a faith in both science and Christianity, who looked for the underlying mechanisms of observable plants and animals. The discoveries made by these genetic, scientific, and medical pioneers have now begun to supplant the miracles of our time. Yet science, medicine, and their underlying philosophies must also recognize their boundaries. Science is very good at studying the mechanisms of the universe, right up to the first few milliseconds after the Big Bang. Yet the first few milliseconds do remain a barrier, and certainly what happened before the Big Bang is unknowable by scientific methods. In a time when belief in the supernatural is at an all-time low, when fake news is "a thing," when Christianity is viewed as a supernatural religion without any of the supernatural, we need to ask: **Is there a supernatural God who is beyond the constraints of the natural world who has done miracles in the past, continues to do miracles in the present, and will do miracles in the future?**

In December of 2015, a friend and former elder at our church fell in his home and was rushed to the hospital. Let's protect his identity and the details of his family by calling him Walter. A series of tests were run, and nothing was found that would contribute to his apparent loss of consciousness—except a series of small structures in his brain revealed by a CT scan. The doctors were uncertain, but their initial diagnosis was that the man had numerous small tumors inside his cranium suggesting multiple neurological pressure points, perhaps sufficient to cause the symptoms he had experienced. More tests were ordered, and the family was prepared for the worst. It was possible that this husband, father, grandfather, retired businessman, and patriarch of the family, had brain cancer that would most certainly kill him. The doctors also offered reassurances that there could be other explanations as well, but once the word cancer had been mentioned, alluded to, hinted at, or proclaimed, not much else could be heard. The children, sons-in-law, grandchildren, and other family members were called and told that it might not be, but maybe could be.... Most arrived at the bedside with worried looks and furrowed brows. Even those who had previously been estranged were there beside the faithful. Walter could not help but be touched and disquieted by their concern. His own brow furrowed, and tears began to fill his eyes as he considered his departure from such a loving family.

Enter the pastor. I arrived just as the crew of people had rallied around Walter. His emotions were just below the surface and his eyes easily misted. My own emotions, caught up in the scene before me, rose to their own crescendo as I considered the implications of losing one of my longtime mentors. I saw the collection of loving and estranged family members, some followers of Jesus, and some who had given up the faith—and I prayed. I prayed for Walter's survival; I prayed that God would remove any and every last cancer cell from his body; I prayed for confident peace for everyone in the room; I prayed for spiritual healing; and I prayed for complete physical healing. When I opened my eyes, I saw the beaming faces of people who appreciated that I had come to pray for this man of God. I recognized that my own pride was definitely getting in the way as I basked in their appreciation just a little too much. I left the hospital with a mix of confidence, joy, sorrow, pride, humility, uncertainty, and perplexity. I believed and asked God to help my unbelief.

A time of waiting ensued. I made it back to the hospital a few days later to find a happy, healthy man and his family. The doctors had done more tests and imaging and had determined that the small tumors seen previously were actually scar tissue from a previous neurological incident. Everyone, including me, was relieved. But, if I am being honest, I also felt a twinge of discomfort. Was this a case of physician incompetence or insensitivity? Why would the doctors have put this man and family through so much anguish if the image was indeed showing scar tissue all along? They must have been reasonably sure of a diagnosis of cancer if they were to suggest that to Walter. It would be irresponsible to be flippant about a cancer diagnosis. Yet they had in fact mentioned it to all concerned. Then **I began to wonder what this situation might have looked like if Walter had indeed had cancer, prayers were prayed, and God answered.**

**Would it not look a lot like this?** I said something to this effect to Walter and we agreed to live with the mystery.

The next day, it was time for staff meeting at the church. I related the story to everyone else on staff. The whole team was indignant with the doctors. People were heard to say, "How could those doctors be so irresponsible and scare this family like that?" "How did they confuse active tumors with scar tissue?" Of course, these were the fleeting questions I had asked in my first moments of hearing the news. The emotions and questions were simply amplified in the setting of multiple leaders building off one another's reactions. What struck me was that no one was thinking of this as a supernatural event. I said this to our staff team, admitting that I had a similar reaction. Why do we so naturally assume that the doctors are right? Why do we so naturally assume that the doctors are wrong? In this case, they would have to be both: wrong about the cancer diagnosis and then right about the scar tissue. What if...? What if...? What if Jesus healed this man? Is that so impossible to believe? It was tough for our staff to believe until we started thinking like this. Church staff (me included) are influenced by the majority culture as well.

Perhaps this story is enough to convince us that we really do need to recapture a sense of the miraculous and supernatural. There is a saying, usually inaccurately attributed to Albert Einstein: "There are only two ways to live your life. One is as though nothing is a miracle. The other is as though everything is." Besides the fact that Einstein never actually said this, the statement is a false dichotomy. I am not suggesting that it would be wise to live as if everything was a miracle, nor would I say that we should live as if nothing was a miracle. Perhaps we could live as if some things are miracles and some things are beautiful gifts from the creator. Take a look at any green plant and know that photosynthesis is happening within it. Take a look at a textbook that shows the biochemical pathways pertaining to photosynthesis. Does this not look like a miracle? Yet it also looks like a natural process built into the warp and woof of the universe. If you put together the right pieces of biological equipment, add carbon dioxide, water, and soil, you get this system that creates energy, water, and oxygen.

J.R.R. Tolkien, the writer of the *Lord of the Rings* books was a realist who believed that God was always at work in the world. [4] Tolkien knew that his stories were fantasy. He knew that the fairies, dwarves, elves, Valar, Balrogs, and other beings he had created were just that, creations of his mind. They have the limited lifespan of his imagination, his books, and the existence of this earth. The lifespans of his creations are great indeed, but limited none-the-less since they are not real. He also knew that humans walk in the world of the earth and the world of the spiritual. Humans are truly supernatural in their scope.

---

[4] J.R.R. Tolkien, *Tolkien on Fairy-stories*, Verlyn Flieger and Douglas A. Anderson; HarperCollins; UK ed. Edition; 2014.

C.S. Lewis, mentored by Tolkien, also knew this. He spoke of humans being amphibians, one-part earthy and one-part spiritual.[5] The purpose of a human's time on earth is to learn to breathe the air of heaven. All of the fairies Tolkien created will pass from this world. God and the image he created in humans will go on for eternity. To Tolkien and Lewis, we are supernatural whether or not we experience anything else supernatural.

In a *Rolling Stone Magazine* interview, Chris Martin of Coldplay said, "I definitely believe in God. How can you look at anything and not be overwhelmed by the miraculousness of it?"[6] He seems to be reiterating the concept that everything is miraculous. In further interviews, we learn that Martin has gone on in the development of his ideas to a place where he refers to himself as all-theistic[7] – he says that he believes in everything. Or perhaps he believes that all things make up god. **But if all is god, if everything is miraculous, does anything catch our attention? Is anything miraculous?**

---

[5] Lewis, C.S. *The Screwtape Letters*. New York: Macmillan Publishing Company, Ltd., 1980, p. 36.
[6] "Coldplay's Quiet Storm," Rolling Stone Magazine, Austin Scaggs, 2005-11-06.
[7] "What is Chris Martin's problem?", Entertainment Music independent.ie. 2008-06-22,
https://www.independent.ie/entertainment/music/what-is-chris-martins-problem-26456889.html, See also Wikipedia: https://en.wikipedia.org/wiki/Chris_Martin

So, for the purposes of this conversation, let us define what we mean by a miracle or the supernatural. Let us say that a miracle is an intervention by the supernatural entity, God. It is God intervening in an otherwise closed system of action and reaction which he also created from the beginning:

> [C.S. Lewis] ... explained that a miracle is something unique that breaks a pattern so expected and established we hardly consider that it could be broken. In his 1947 *Miracles*, he wrote, "Men became scientific because they expected law in nature and they expected law in nature because they believed in a lawgiver." That is why most of the great founding fathers of modern science believed in an order. Scientists, a few of which include Galileo (astronomy), Newton (calculus), Mendel (genetics) and Einstein (physics), were convinced that an order existed and pursued the search for it. In essence, science is the discovery or clarification of an order that reveals God in nature.[8]

---

[8] "Miracles and Why We're Reluctant to Own Them," Jane Simon, M.D., Huffpost, The Blog, 2016-11-07, https://www.huffingtonpost.com/jane-simon-md/miracles-and-why-were-rel_b_12798488.html.

God establishes order by which the universe functions, and that order was evident in the first few micro-seconds after the Big Bang, as most scientists would agree, and in the first few moments after creation as the theologically-attuned person would say.[9] God created the universe and also created the principles of physics, math, chemistry, and biology in which the universe operates. But God reserves the right to enter into his creation and be the external cause of reactions here in time and space. It is this entering in and becoming a first cause by the creator God, that qualifies as a miracle.

God has given us several examples of his intervention in the Bible. Jesus calmed a storm as described in Mark 4:35-41.[10] God established a system, whereby winds and storms happen on the surface of our planet. The trade winds of a continent, the local geographic features, the heat of the sun, the evaporation of water from local rivers and lakes, all affect the natural wind and weather of an area. These naturally occurring events had all come together to create a storm on the sea of Galilee which Jesus then calmed. The Gospel of Mark does not describe how Jesus calmed the storm. Could it have been that he had the power to equalize the

---

[9] I do not wish to confuse issues at this point by getting into a debate about the Big Bang and Creation. It is sufficient to say that I see no contradiction between the Creation of God as described in the Bible and the Big Bang model of the universe.
[10] (Holy Bible New Living Translation 2012), all references to the Bible will be from this version unless otherwise stated.

differential barometric pressures of two parts of the natural world and the wind settled down? Perhaps at the same time he dispersed the clouds and allowed the sun to shine on the lake? Did Jesus speed up the weather processes on the lake and cause the storm to pass quickly? If Jesus is master of time and nature, he may have other mechanisms available that we would not even comprehend. But here is the important part, we are told that it was indeed an intervention by the miraculous power of Jesus. No human has this kind of power to change the course of the wind and weather established by God at creation. Mark tells us that Jesus has this power.

A young girl who had died, her body in the middle of a funeral lament, was brought back to life by this same Jesus (Luke 8:40-56). A man born blind was healed such that he could see (John 9:2-3). Water miraculously became wine in vessels never designed to contain wine (John 2:1-11). These all represent interventions by the deity who is the great creator, acting through the person of Jesus. They are not common. We do not know their mechanism and they are not the kind of thing that happens by the intervention of humans. They point to a higher authority.

After Jesus had died, risen from the dead (the definitive miracle for all time), and left the earth, miracles continued to happen by the power of his name. We are told about lame people who, at the name of Jesus, were able to walk (Acts 3:1-11 and Acts 9:32-35), prisoners whose chains fell off their arms and locked iron gates that swung open (Acts 12:6-19), the premature death of persons who were irreverent toward Jesus and tried to deceive the disciples (Acts 5:1-11 and Acts 12:20-23), and the survival of Paul when he was bitten by a deadly snake (Acts 28:3-6). All through church history, before and after the process of gathering the books of the Bible into a whole canon, there have been testimonies of God's miraculous intervention into his otherwise closed system of cause and reaction. Sometimes he acts on his own and sometimes he acts in response to the prayers of people.

There might be other ways in which miracles could happen, other agents, other demons, other angels, but here in this context, we will limit our thoughts to miracles in which God is the prime intervenor. When we speak of miracles, we will endeavor to consider events that match this type of intervention from God as distinct from common acts of chemistry, biology, and physics. For those of us who read the Bible for spiritual enlightenment and growth, it is these miracles that sustain our faith and it is miracles such as these for which we will look in our contemporary world. We have a sense that God is behind all of the natural and supernatural events of the universe and even other universes if they exist.

So, in the chapters to come we will explore a "thought experiment" on why God does not reveal himself more clearly, I will reveal why I am so interested in the topic, and we will sketch out the barest of theologies regarding miracles. Chapter Five will recount stories of miracles I have come across in researching this book, and Chapter Six will tell of the miracles of Celtic Christianity. We will then go on to look at the relationship between science and the supernatural, talk about how difficult it is to have a conversation about miracles that happened, and in Chapter Nine, speak of the ways in which the supernatural has broken into the Church in recent history. Chapters Ten through Thirteen provide guidance for our imagination as we consider the supernatural, speak of the disappointment of not seeing answers to prayer, suggest ways in which we long for something more than just the material world, and consider how we, in light of all we have shared, might choose to live in this world. So, I suggest you buckle your seatbelt and get ready for experiences and miracles that will challenge your mind as well as your emotions. Let's explore the world of the supernatural together.

## Chapter 2: A Thought Experiment

I have a friend (let's call him Robert) who has lost the ability to see. No, his eyes work fine, but he no longer knows how to see the miracles and mysteries around him. With regard to the statement, "There are only two ways to live your life. One is as though nothing is a miracle. The other is as though everything is," he would say *nothing* is a miracle. The way he now sees things is that there are no such things as miracles, and all can be explained by science without a creator. He was not always this way. He is one who at various points in his life has been a leader in the church, a member of the board of a church, a leader in a pastors' group, and a fund-raiser for a Christian organization. His last prayer to God was, "God, I am struggling with my faith, I don't know if I believe in you anymore; if you don't show me you exist, I am going to leave this faith and become an atheist." God did not *show* Robert that he exists and today, Robert would say that there are several reasons he left the faith. He struggles with finding sufficient evidence to support the claims of the Bible; he struggles with the punishment of God and other things that have driven him to his position. He and I continue to talk about this and will not easily find agreement but, for now, I want to focus on one part of Robert's journey because it is one that affects many people. That is, **I want to focus on why God doesn't reveal himself more clearly.**

On one hand, Robert's statement to God sounds like a reasonable thing to do. He was asking God to prove that he is there. It is the equivalent of a man named Gideon who lived approximately 3200 years ago. Gideon, we are told in the book of Judges in the Old Testament of the Christian Bible (Judges 6:33-40), was hiding from his enemies in Ophrah, near the valley of Jezreel, west of the Jordan River at a time when the Midianite people were trying hard to take back the land that God had given to Israel. The Midianites would regularly raid the fields and livestock of the Israelite people leaving them destitute and hungry. One day, an angel of the Lord greeted Gideon and said, "Mighty hero, the Lord is with you!" Gideon, who does not seem to be afraid of angels, gives a surly reply, "Hah, if God is with us, why has all of this happened to us? If God is for us, why am I hiding in this winepress harvesting a bit of grain to feed my family? Where are all of the miracles we used to see?" He is quite plainly asking for a miracle. It is much like my friend Rob saying, "God, why is my life so difficult? I really don't think you are on my side. I want you to show me that you are there."

In Gideon's case, the angel replies, "You are the one who is going to rescue your people." But before the angel leaves, God proves that he is with Gideon with a supernatural miracle. Gideon brings out an offering of meat and soaks it in broth and the angel touches it with his walking stick and turns it to ashes. Wow, what a miracle! An angel ignites his offering to God and turns it into carbon molecules. Surely Gideon is ready to do anything God asks him to do. Well, no. The next time we see Gideon we find him asking for further proof that God is with him. God has promised to make him the leader of an army that will defeat their enemies and Gideon says, "Um, excuse me but, God, if I am going to lead an army for you, I need some proof. I would like you to do something for me. I am going to put a sheep's skin out on the ground and go to bed. While I sleep, I would like you to make the wool wet and the ground dry." God, in one of the greatest condescensions of all time, says that he will do this. In the morning, there is proof that God is with Gideon: the fleece is wet, and the ground is dry. But Gideon, who shows himself to be very difficult to convince, asks for still another sign that God is with him. "Uh, God, one more little thing, I realized that a wet lamb skin and dry ground might just be coincidence. Could you just reverse that and make the ground wet and the fleece dry? I promise, this is my last request." God obliges and so Gideon, after three miraculous signs, is finally convinced that God is with him and that God wants him to lead the Israelite army. It seems that Gideon is even more difficult to convince than my friend Robert. Robert would likely have been satisfied with the first display of power.

Yet Robert's ultimatum is ultimately unfair to God, and dangerous to himself. Let's use a thought experiment to explain why his demand can never be completely answered in the way that Robert wants it to be answered. For the purposes of this thought experiment, let us say that God did reveal himself in a miraculous way to Robert. If God walked into Robert's home in a bodily form and said something to him that only Robert and God could know; that would certainly meet the requirements of showing Robert that God existed. But, would it really satisfy Robert? Suppose a few days after God showed up in his home, Robert began to ask questions, as most of us would. He might think, "Hmm, I wonder if that really happened or did I just imagine it? Was I wanting so badly for something to happen that I hallucinated about God walking into my house?" Or he might think, "Did someone find a way to trick me into thinking God showed up in my home? Was that someone in a costume who found inside information?" He might go down a different path of logic, "Could that have been an alien from another planet that showed up in my house? Could he read my mind?" Like Gideon, Robert might soon be asking for one more proof that God existed. Would a further appearance or miraculous event convince Robert?

Beyond the reasonable doubts (or even unreasonable doubts) that would likely arise for Robert, there are other problems. If Robert could be convinced beyond any doubt that God existed, he would find himself in an exceptional situation. He would now know that the great creator of the universe actually did exist. He would no longer be living by faith, he would be living by sight. Life would no longer be about trusting an unseen God, but rather, seeking to please a known entity. Every word from his mouth, every action he took would need to be assessed in light of his new knowledge. **Instead of Robert being able to trust and show love in a genuine manner, he might feel conscripted or forced to love this creator who had placed him upon the earth.** This kind of knowledge might lead Rob to feel like a robot without freewill to do as he chose. Rob's world would become a theocracy with God as the absolute king of his life with little room for finding his own way in that life.

Then there would be the problem of what to do with the information Robert had. If Robert now knew that God existed, would he not feel a responsibility to let others know about this God who had revealed himself to him? How would he go about telling others about his experience? Who would believe that the God of the universe had actually revealed himself to Robert? Robert would likely now feel he needed to call upon God again and ask him to reveal himself to others in a similar manner. Eventually, God would have to reveal himself to others if this whole process was to work. Soon, every single person on the planet would need their own special visit from the God of the universe. And soon, the whole world would be caught up in the theocracy in which Robert found himself.

C.S. Lewis knew this problem all too well and writes of it in his magnificent work, *The Screwtape Letters*. In this book, Screwtape, a demon (or sticking to Lewis' terminology, a devil) in charge of training other demons, calls God "the Enemy" and counsels his junior demon on how to tempt and mislead a human. Screwtape explains why God does not make it clearer that he exists by use of the supernatural:

> You must have often wondered why the Enemy does not make more use of His power to be sensibly present to human souls in any degree He chooses and at any moment. But you now see that the Irresistible and the Indisputable are the two weapons which the very nature of His scheme forbids Him to use. Merely to over-ride a human will (as His felt presence in any but the faintest and most mitigated degree would certainly do) would be for Him useless. He cannot ravish. He can only woo.[11]

Lewis wrote these words in 1942 and they still have weight today. **They describe a God who has chosen to make himself resistible. He will woo humans but will not force them to submit to his will and therefore he will not reveal himself in a way that makes him irresistible.**

Wendell Berry says something similar in his book, *Jayber Crow*, and perhaps better explains how even the

---

[11] Lewis, C.S. *The Screwtape Letters*. New York: MacMillan Publishing Co., Inc, 1980, p. 38, 39.

"faintest and mitigated" presence of God would override human will. Berry says:

> Christ did not descend from the cross except into the grave. And why not otherwise? Wouldn't it have put fine comical expressions on the faces of the scribes and chief priests and the soldiers if at that moment He had come down in power and glory? Why didn't He do it? Why hasn't He done it at any one of a thousand good times between then and now? …. He didn't, He hasn't, because from the moment He did, He would be the absolute tyrant of the world and we would be His slaves. Even those who hated Him and hated one another and hated their own souls would have to believe in Him then. From that moment the possibility that we might be bound to Him and He to us and us to one another by love forever would be ended. … Those who wish to see Him must see Him in the poor, the hungry, the hurt, the wordless creatures, the groaning and travailing beautiful world.[12]

---

[12] Wendell Berry, *Jayber Crow*, Counterpoint, 2001, p. 173-174.

In the thought experiment I have described in which my friend Robert and others in the world get a direct visitation from God, Berry is suggesting that the resulting relationship with God would be one of slavery and power. God's revelations of the best ways to live would become commands that needed to be obeyed by all and resisted by none. Instead, God has chosen to make himself resistible, for we must trust that he is there. Our relationship with him becomes one of love and trust with the Creator of the universe. As Wendell Berry is suggesting, it results in a world in which we must seek to find God. We seek him in the midst of our questions, our doubts, our longing for a better world. We seek him in creation, we seek him in humanity that bears his image, we seek him as we help one another find him, we seek him in joy, we seek him in pain, and we seek him as we try to live out this trust in a God who calls us, yet does not force himself upon us.

So, while this book is about the supernatural, and I am hopeful that it might lead some to consider trusting God, **I am not seeking to *prove* once and for all that a supernatural world exists or that miracles still happen or ever did happen**. Because of how God has created the universe and how he chooses to interact with humans, such a thing would not be possible. I have already told stories of things that are worthy of being called supernatural miracles and I will relate yet more in this book, but one will readily see that none of the miracles that are related in this book will ever prove their truth to any audience beyond the one who experienced the miracle. Even the person who experiences the miracle may not be entirely persuaded that they have witnessed a supernatural event. Those who experience a miracle may feel for a time that their miracle is a proof of a supernatural world and the power of God, but **even the most amazing miracle fades with time and we find ourselves wondering if it happened or if we interpreted it correctly**. Certainly, a miracle experienced by one person is difficult to communicate to another and so we will readily find ourselves questioning the authenticity of supernatural events related by others. We weren't there, and we don't know the people who tell the story, and so there is great difficulty in knowing whether or not we should trust someone else's word on such things as miracles.

So, if I am not trying to *prove* the existence of a supernatural world, what is the purpose of this book? I do hope that this book might contribute to the discussion. I pray that it might allow us to begin to ask the questions and that we might begin to look for supernatural events in our world. **I believe that if we look for miracles, we just might see them, and we might indeed be convinced—not in a provable way, but in a faith sort of way—that there is more to the world in which we live than things that can be detected with our five senses and measured with the instruments of science.** I will talk more later about miracles and their purpose, but for now, I am hoping to seed a small amount of faith in the minds of those who are steeped in naturalism and closed to faith.

Many in our world are being convinced, by scientism and naturalism, that there is nothing else to this world. They, like Bart Campolo, no longer believe in the supernatural religions of the world. They have lost their ability to see beyond their five senses and so they do not believe in anything that does not fit this perspective. This leaves them closed to the possibility of anything beyond the physical world. It excludes any concept of God and prevents them from responding to God in faith. The natural world becomes their god and naturalism becomes their religion. The voices of science and naturalism have become so strong in our world that they are largely drowning out any voices that speak of a supernatural world. Can we once again open our minds to a worldview in which miracles can occur? Can we even accept the miracles that we may have experienced in our own lives? For when they consider all of their experiences, and are open to such assessment, many people will recount some experience that makes them think there may be something beyond what can be measured by science. This book is a call to consider, or consider again, a worldview that allows for God to interact with his ordered creation.

C.S. Lewis often resorted to metaphor and allusion to allow the reader to explore complex concepts and the relation between the physical world and the supernatural world. He was a master of logical discourse but did not limit himself to speaking and persuading by such means. I have already referred to his classic story of "devils" in the service of Satan in which a senior devil instructs a junior devil in the art of temptation – *The Screwtape Letters* – and I will do so again here after reminding the reader of the inverted sense in which we must read this quote. Remember, God is called "The Enemy" and Satan is called "Our Father" by Screwtape. Lewis used a few sentences to explain the concept of humans who live in both a physical and a spiritual world:

> Humans are amphibians – half spirit and half animal. (The Enemy's determination to produce such a revolting hybrid was one of the things that determined Our Father to withdraw his support from Him.) As spirits, they belong to the eternal world, but as animals they inhabit time. This means that while their spirit can be directed to an eternal object, their bodies, passions, and imaginations are in continual change, for to be in time means to change.[13]

Lewis is suggesting that there is a "flaw" in our human structure, and it can be exploited by the devil. This flaw is our amphibious nature and the fact that we live in

---

[13] Lewis, C.S. *The Screwtape Letters*. New York: Macmillan Publishing Company, Ltd., 1980, p. 36.

two worlds. *I am suggesting* **that as a culture, and as individuals, we may be losing the ability to live in two worlds or, more specifically, losing our ability to live in the spiritual world.** Our spiritual lungs are atrophying while our physical "gills" are taking over and doing all the work. In this state, our spiritual lungs will never be able to live in the rarified air of the supernatural world and we will be doomed to hover in this imperfect physical world forever. The rest of this book will be dedicated to challenging our loss of the supernatural in our day-to-day lives and encouraging us to develop our spiritual lungs.

## Chapter 3: Why Me, Lord?

The reader might ask, "Why is this author so interested in miracles? What has happened in his life to suggest that miracles even happen?" I would say there are two things that spur me on in this direction. First, there is the fact that almost everyone seems to have either a miracle story from their own life, or at least a "spooky coincidence" story that gives them pause to ask whether or not it was indeed a coincidence. Second, there are my own supernatural experiences.

The story of my most significant miracle starts in the spring of 2007. It was one of the most convincing times where I saw God at work in answering the prayers of his people. In March, I began having some pain in the right side of my face. The pain radiated in three swaths: one near my temple, one near my eye-socket, and a third band of pain close to my jawline, all on the right side. My doctor soon told me that this kind of pain was consistent with something called trigeminal neuralgia. A bit of research gave me the information I needed to understand what might be going on. In trigeminal neuralgia, a nerve gets inflamed and sends pain signals to the brain. The fifth cranial nerve, which derives from the pons, located at the base of the brain, provides sensory information from three regions of the face. Schematic drawings I found on medical websites confirmed that the three regions served by the fifth cranial nerve were the same as the regions of excruciating pain on the right side of my face. Some of the information was not very encouraging. Articles informed me that some people go through long periods of their lives experiencing this pain. Some experience it all the time while others find that it comes and goes. For those with specific episodes of trigeminal neuralgia, it may be brought on by something as benign as the draft from an air-conditioning system blowing on their face. Some articles called the pain associated with this condition "suicide pain" since some people had felt so debilitated by the severe pain that they chose to take their own lives. I began to pray that the continual recurrence of this pain would not be my lot in life.

As my doctor continued to investigate, a CT scan indicated a mass on the pons of my brain. No one wants to hear the word "mass" on any portion of the brain. The pons, a portion of the brainstem buried deep within the skull and part of the brain stem, is the place from which the trigeminal nerve begins. A mass impinging upon this portion of the brain certainly fit with the symptoms I was experiencing. Could this be the source of my pain? Other questions would need to be asked and answered. Was this a cancerous lesion? Was this something that might grow? Was this something that could kill me? Many questions and fears went through my mind and the mind of my wife as we did our best to trust God with the future. The doctor did tell me that the spot where this mass was residing was a surgical "no go" zone. There would be no way to remove this bit of tissue without damaging large portions of my brain. If this was a cancerous tumour, then other, non-surgical methods of treatment would be required. I could tell by the expression on her face that none of the other treatments would be very promising.

I remember experiencing a number of emotions as I left the doctor's office that day. As I drove back to work, I remember asking questions like, "Is this the moment in which I must face my own mortality? **Could this tiny mass on the pons of my brain be the thing that ushers me out of this world?**" I remember having quite a conversation with God that day, which ramped up and down through a range of emotions. But at the end of the prayer (or perhaps it was more of a rant) I remember saying to God, "Alright, if this is either something with which I must live or something with which I must die, I will trust you, Lord. I commit myself to praising you even with my last breath." Those were brave words even if I was unclear how well I might live up to them. I was very much aware that I might turn into a whiner who complained about how unfair all of this was, yet I was trying to give this situation every bit of my faith and commitment to Jesus. Only time would tell how well I would live up to such valiant remarks.

This brought me to a period of waiting for an MRI, a better form of imaging for the structures of the brain. During this period of waiting, my wife and I asked a few faithful people of prayer to pray that God would take away the pain and remove anything that might be causing the pain. We committed ourselves to praying for effective medical remedies and for the miraculous intervention of the God of the universe. People did pray for healing. We went on about the daily rhythms of life and took time to enjoy a vacation even as the doctors loaded me up with pain killers that should have been enough to tranquilize a horse. Then on about April 10th the pain began to subside. At first it was just a small change in intensity, but then I began to notice a significant trend of less and less pain. Over the next four weeks, the pain had slowly but steadily dwindled to nothing and never returned again.

On Monday, May 7th I had an MRI and the next day my doctor gave me the results. The MRI results showed an absolutely normal brain. The pons looked typical, there was no evidence of a mass of any sort and as far as they could tell, there was nothing abnormal in my brain. Whatever the CT scan had previously shown, it was no longer there. The doctor began to say things like, "There must have been an artefact on the original CT results." It was almost an apology for a false alarm. Still, I couldn't help but think of the fact that when they saw the mass (or artefact), I had been experiencing intense pain. Then, when no mass could be detected, there was no pain. I told the doctor that a number of people had prayed for my healing and she brushed it off as superstition and coincidence. I couldn't blame her; I did not know what to think either. Still, every time I think about the series of events, I am left with questions and hints that point toward a genuine miracle. I had agonising pain that led me to seek help. The doctors saw what they thought was a tumour in my brain. I asked people to pray for a resolution and the pain and the mass went away. It would seem that a brain tumour disappeared by some means unknown to medical practitioners. **If God chose to miraculously heal someone, is this not what it would look like from a medical, scientific perspective?** We will never *know* for sure – that is why it is called a life of faith – but this certainly has all of the indications of a miracle.

I am aware that it is hard for anyone who reads these words to conclude with me that this may have been a miracle. There are factors that make it hard to believe. The reader must ask questions about my character and trustworthiness. They might wonder if the writer is seeking to deceive people for fame or book sales. The rarity of such events means that most of us have not experienced a chain of events like those I have described. Those who hear my story will never be able to assess how intense the pain was. They may be left wondering if I imagined the whole thing. Was it psychosomatic in nature? I would have the same questions in listening to someone else's miracle story. **Yet, is it not also possible that there are things beyond our natural world? Is it not also possible that God occasionally reaches into his creation and does something extraordinary?** Could it be that the doctor, a few praying friends, my wife, and I experienced one such miracle in this world?

I have chosen to view this whole incident as a miraculous healing and refer to it from time-to-time in my own mind when I find that my faith in God may be beginning to wane. This healing has become a touchstone moment in my life. It is often a significant encouragement for me to pray fervently for healing in other people's lives and reminds me of the spiritual power available to us when we pray.

The next questions my reader and I must ask are related to what this means about the nature of healings. Rather than this miracle being a "feather in my cap" that suggests I am someone special and that God chose to heal me, I would suggest that it becomes a humbling experience, raising more questions. One such question would be, **"Why would I receive such a miracle when so many others around me have not?"**

At the time of this incident in my life, I was praying weekly for my good friend Jason (this is not his real name and many of the rest of the names in this book have been changed to protect their privacy) who was undergoing treatment for multiple myeloma. Multiple myeloma is a form of bone cancer in which plasma cells are overproduced in the bone marrow. This overproduction leads to the destruction of bones and to the crowding out of other healthy blood cells. At the height of his illness, the bones in Jason's body were riddled with holes like Swiss cheese and the cancer cells were draining him of energy. Another friend and I met weekly with Jason seeking God's wisdom in prayer, praying for each other, praying for healing, asking for forgiveness of sin, praying for other issues in our own lives and in the lives of people with whom we interacted. We did this for several years and although Jason went through all of the procedures of chemotherapy, bone marrow transplant, and several other experimental techniques, Jason never got his healing. Well, that is not completely true. More accurately, I should say, Jason never got a quick or instantaneous healing of all of his symptoms here on earth. His life was extended significantly longer than the doctors had predicted and ultimately, those of us who have a faith in heavenly realms believe that his body is now completely healed as he resides with Jesus in heaven. In fact, we have hope that he has been given a new body without any of the frailties he experienced here on earth. The damage done by years of playing squash has been reversed, the loss of hair from his bald pate has been replenished, and he is a new man as he carries out whatever work God has for him in the Kingdom of God beyond this world.

But—and here is the big question: Why didn't Jason get the same kind of healing I am ascribing to myself? Is it a matter of things God has for each of us to do here on earth? Am I slower to complete my tasks and so God healed me so that I could do more here on earth? For what purpose here on earth could Jesus be calling me, and giving me a healing that surpasses the healing my friend was able to experience? What about another friend of mine who lives every day in a wheelchair because of a traffic accident two decades ago? Why hasn't he received his miracle here on earth? The questions pile up one upon another to the point where I would sometimes like to say that I did not receive a miracle at all. I want to simply say, "My doctor was right, there was an artefact on the image from the CT scan." But, if the disappearance of my tumour and my pain was a supernatural event, what then? If I ascribe my healing to an artefact on a CT scan, am I not in serious danger of crediting something other than God for a tremendously significant event in my life? We know how sad it makes us when someone else gets the credit for work we have done. What are we saying to God when we ignore his work in our lives and give something or someone else the credit?

As you can readily gather, there are still many questions about this experience, and this is the way we would expect it to be. **God never wraps his miracles in tidy packages covered with coloured paper and ribbons.** He does not explain all of the details. He leaves us wondering. He leaves us questioning. He leaves us with room for faith and room for doubt. He calls us to faith and asks us to be motivated by faith. He calls us to greater leadership and greater purposes in his will for this planet and the people around us. He asks us to believe that the miracles that happen are his way of inspiring us to greater heights. He woos us and calls us to enter into his grand work. He does not enslave us.

The Bible tells us that the "prayer offered in faith will heal the sick, and the Lord will make them well" (James 5:15). Notice, it does not say that the person praying makes them well. It says that the person is to offer prayer in faith and that the Lord will make them well. It encourages us to "pray for each other so that [we] may be healed [because] … the earnest prayer of a righteous person has great power and wonderful results" (James 5:16). He has not promised that He will heal in every circumstance and he has not said that he will explain all things this side of heaven. He asks us to trust and rely on him to give us sufficient answers for the moment and more complete answers at another time. He tells us that the best we can expect right now is to see things dimly like we are looking through a distorted or cloudy mirror. Take a look at 1 Corinthians 13:11-13:

> When I was a child, I spoke and thought and reasoned as a child. But when I grew up, I put away childish things. Now we see things imperfectly, like puzzling reflections in a mirror, but then we will see everything with perfect clarity. All that I know now is partial and incomplete, but then I will know everything completely, just as God now knows me completely. Three things will last forever—faith, hope, and love—and the greatest of these is love.

That certainly makes it sound like we must wait for final answers. Today, as I look once again at these incidents from my own life, I find myself gladly saying things that sound much like those who we see healed by Jesus in the New Testament writings, "I don't know but, praise God, I'm healed!" (See, for example, Luke 17:15 and many more instances from the time Jesus was on the earth).

As we look at the miracles of Jesus in the New Testament, also known as signs and wonders, it is apparent that sometimes the miracles Jesus performed were obvious enough to be available for many to see. And there were also times when people were in the vicinity of the miracle and were unaware that anything unusual had taken place. Think of his first miraculous sign in which he turned water into wine (John 2). There were many present for the wedding but only a few knew that Jesus had turned water into wine. The disciples of Jesus knew and Jesus' mother knew, but most of the guests did not. Significantly, it also seems that the bridegroom did not know and certainly, the "master of the banquet" had no idea of the source of this choice wine. Yes, there are times when a large crowd is aware of the miracle performed. In John 6:14 we read that most of the 5000 people fed by five loaves of bread and two fish understood that a great miracle had taken place. Yet many of the signs performed by Jesus were witnessed by only a select few who told others about the event.

In contemporary times, how often might someone witness a miracle that only a few see? As I think of my own life, I realize there have also been a handful of events that I see as miracles or circumstances that leave me wondering if they might have been miracles. I will relate a few of these stories that leave me scratching my head.

For example, several years ago there was a particular "exotic dancer bar" in northwest Calgary. My route to and from certain retail stores took me past this place. I had seen provocatively-dressed young women come out of the bar and get into the trucks of long-haul drivers as they made their way through town. I made an educated guess about what was going on and then I committed myself to praying for justice in this situation every time I drove past the place. I began to pray that God would shut down any illegal activity or anything that would be harmful to the women who worked there. Two weeks later the business closed down. **Was that one of Jesus' quiet miracles? Or was it just a coincidence? That is a question I will not be able to answer this side of heaven. Yet it inspires me to pray more of these prayers.**

A few years later, my wife and I moved to Vancouver and I was told of a local bar that featured an annual anti-Christmas party that mocked Jesus. So, I again decided to bring this situation to God in prayer. A few weeks later the owners could no longer run the business and it shut down. Was this a quiet miracle or another coincidence? Again, the data is insufficient, and I cannot say.

How many other things might Jesus do around the world that go unnoticed by all but a few individuals? Are they less of a miracle because they are seen by only a few? Are there other incidents that I have witnessed without knowing that Jesus intervened? Were they a miracle that only someone else could understand?

In the gospel of John we are told that Jesus performed miracles as signs of his glory (John 2:11). Our Western world needs to see some miracles that will point to the glory of Jesus. Our eyes need to be open and aware of what is happening around us so that we do not miss the miracles that may already be happening. Can I challenge you, the reader, to watch for a miracle today? Certainly, if you see something, get in touch with me or someone else and talk about it.

## Chapter 4: A Theology of Miracles

Despite the title of this chapter, it is not my intention to give a thorough and systematic theology of miracles. First, I do not have the education required to do that sort of work; second, others have already done that work; and third, it is too large of a study to be included in this book. What I do want to do in this chapter is to give us an understanding of some of the theological debates, how people have determined a position on the nature of the supernatural and miracles, and state my own understanding at this point in my life. If the reader wishes to better understand a theology of miracles, writers such as C.S. Lewis (*Miracles*, 1947),[14] Gordon Fee (*The Disease of the Health & Wealth Gospels*, 2006),[15] and Craig S. Keener (*Miracles, The Credibility of the New Testament Accounts*, 2 volumes, 2011)[16] would be good places to start.

Thomas Aquinas, the great Doctor of the Church, who lived prior to the separation of the Catholic and Protestant churches (1225-1274), believed in miracles and defined them as "something difficult and unusual, surpassing the capabilities of nature and the expectations of those who wonder at it."[17] Years later, when the

---

[14] (Lewis 2015)
[15] (Fee 2006)
[16] (Keener 2011)
[17] Augustine, *De utilitate credendi*, 16. PL 42, 90

separation of Catholic and Protestant churches was a reality, Pope Benedict XIV (1675-1758), suggested that "a miracle need be only above the powers of corporeal creatures."[18] What he was saying was that indeed miracles occur and they are something accomplished by God or one of his created spiritual beings. There has been much debate as to the nature of miracles for all of the history of the church and, to deal with the necessary questions related to miracles, Catholic theology has developed stringent tests designed to assess whether or not an event is a legitimate miracle. This process of verifying miracles is of particular importance to the Catholic Church since part of their theology rests on knowing which of the "saints" are truly in heaven. The thought is that if Catholics can know who is in heaven, they can pray to them and ask for their intercession with God. **Thus, we do well to consider the stringent approach of the Catholic Church as they seek to determine whether or not a miracle is real.** The majority of the miracles investigated by the Catholic Church are medical miracles, and so there is a usual process for such miracles. The process involves teams of medical doctors and theologians who travel to the scene of the event and investigate the supposed miracle to determine the true facts and see if they are consistent with a medical healing or a miraculous healing. The doctors are the first to examine the miracle before a team of theologians does the same. Then both doctors and theologians discuss among themselves the

---

[18] De servorum Dei beatificatione et beatorum canonizatione

legitimacy and all the facts surrounding the miracles before drawing a conclusion.[19]

According to Dr. Edgardo Yordan of the International Medical Committee of Lourdes, the process involves the following considerations. The supposed miracle must involve a lethal condition (a characteristic so stringent that even some of the miracles of the Bible would not qualify). The healing must be instantaneous or happen over a reasonably short period of time. The healing must be lasting and complete and it must be clear that no medical intervention played a part in the cure.[20] It would be interesting to have such a team examine my own healing miracle and hear their assessment, but alas, I am not a Catholic and I did not pray to a saint to ask for healing. Catholic catechisms speak of faith being in accordance with reason, and that our logical minds may seek external proofs that can be joined with the Holy Spirit in giving us confidence in the miracles of God.[21] Thus,

---

[19] Patrick Kelly, executive director of the Blessed John Paul II Shrine in Washington, as quoted in "Late Pope John Paul II to get sainthood, Vatican says," Hada Messia, CNN, 2013, https://edition.cnn.com/2013/07/05/world/europe/vatican-pope-sainthood/index.html

[20] (Yordan 2017)

[21] "that the submission of our faith might nevertheless be in accordance with reason, God willed that external proofs of his Revelation should be joined to the internal helps of the Holy Spirit." Thus the miracles of Christ and the saints, prophecies, the Church's growth and holiness, and her fruitfulness and stability "are the most certain signs of divine Revelation,

Catholic theologians have spent many years developing a theology of miracles and we do well to pay attention to their conclusions.

Of course, Catholics are not the only ones to consider the nature of miracles and what constitutes a miracle. There are a wide range of philosophical and theological positions on the nature of miracles. For the purposes of this book we will list and briefly discuss a few of these varying positions.

A good place to start is Deism. Deism is a concept that allows for the existence of God and suggests that God created the universe, wound it up like a watch, and let it go. Thus, Deism still has a place for a God who created the universe but asserts that God never interacts with his creation beyond the natural structures he created that sustain the universe. In this philosophical construct, miracles do not and never did happen. People may observe the happenings of the universe and interpret something as a miracle, but if all could be known about the situation, it would readily be seen that the events were simple cause and reaction as intended by the creator God who set the universe in motion.

---

adapted to the intelligence of all" Catechism of the Catholic Church, Chapter three: Man's Response to God, Article 1, III, The Characteristics of Faith,
https://www.catholicculture.org/culture/library/catechism/index.cfm?recnum=92

It is hard to distinguish such a theological approach to miracles, from the philosophical position of Empiricism, which does not allow for a creator. In Deism, God is there but he really does not interact with his creation. Such an approach may leave some disinterested in God and there is little reason to approach God in this construct that leads to a view of God that is akin to "destiny" or "fate."

Next, we might give a short description of Cessationism. I am intentionally painting with broad strokes in this chapter and so I will simply say that **Cessationism is a theological construct that suggests that at one time, God did do miracles and led his people by signs and wonders, but that he no longer needs to do miracles and we cannot expect them to happen in our time.** There are a number of ways in which people come to such a conclusion and so there is much overlap with other theological positions, but we will keep things simple for the purposes of this book. The most usual form of Cessationism would say that miracles were necessary in Old Testament times and in the early years after the resurrection of Christ but that once the Canon of the Bible had been established, and the printing press allowed for the dissemination of the words of those who experienced the resurrection, there was no longer a need for miracles—and miracles ceased. Many ascribe to some form of Cessationism either formally or implicitly. Even some who claim to believe that God can still do miracles today would fall into a category of functional cessationist because they tend to explain away the supernatural in other ways. Many in the Evangelical church fall into this category and give lip-service to miracles but are hard-pressed to point to anything that they would call a genuine miracle.

Deism and Cessationism both rule out the possibility of the miraculous occurring now in the 21st Century. They are popular ideas in the Western world and much less popular in the Southern Hemisphere and developing world. Those cultures have a greater openness to the supernatural and more readily embrace the possibility of God's divine intervention. I wonder if God is ever amused by our theological debates about such things. **It seems that throughout history when groups of people have nearly completely ruled out the supernatural, God once again breaks into time and space and breaks open the comfortable theological boxes we have created to contain our belief in Empiricism.**

On the other end of the spectrum of miraculous expectation is something that, for the sake of clarity, I will call "hyper-supernaturalism." There are those who anticipate that God will do multiple miracles per day in a single individual's life if we just create the right environment and systems in which he will work. Some evangelistic and revival meetings of the past and present seek to create an environment in which sufficient faith is present for God to heal the sick and do other miracles. We have likely all met some fellow Christian who tries to convince us of everyday miracles such as finding a downtown parking spot where none existed until they mouthed a simple prayer. They speak of gas reserves that last well beyond the empty mark on their cars as a sign that God answered their prayer to get them to their destination, or the person who showed up with a can of gas just as they had begun to think there was no hope of them being found with their empty tank.

In this system, there is a degree of pressure placed upon those who seek a miracle to have a level of faith equal to the miracle they seek from God. Many have gone away from such meetings believing that the reason a miracle did not happen was because of a lack of faith: either their own lack, or the lack of others at the meeting. One particular version of this hyper-supernaturalism is sometimes known as the "prosperity gospel." In this version, it is God's will that all sickness, death, and poverty cease to exist in the here and now of this world. We can admire and sympathize with those who desire to see a large outpouring of the miraculous in our present day but if we do believe that God functions in this way, we must ask why it is that so much pain, suffering, and poverty still do exist in our world. If God wills that all might be healed and be free of need, why do we continue to see a world with any misery? I again refer the reader to others who have worked out a theology related to the miraculous and in particular the prosperity gospel. In particular, one could look to Dr. Gordon Fee's book *The Disease of the Health and*

*Wealth Gospel.*[22] Here I will agree with Dr. Fee and simply say that a position of hyper-supernaturalism does not seem tenable in our present world.

Perhaps at this point, it would be good to take a few minutes to deal with a common response in which some would say that the reason there is still misery in the world is because people do not have enough faith. Those who wish to argue this will sometimes refer us to Matthew 17:14-20 where Jesus criticizes those present (or is he criticizing all of humanity?) because of their lack of faith: "You faithless and corrupt people! How long must I be with you? How long must I put up with you? Bring the boy here to me." (Matthew 17:17). Wow, those are some of the harshest words used by Jesus, especially as we consider that his disciples had just tried to heal the young man in question. Jesus goes on to "rebuke a demon" and "make the boy well." You might rightly ask me if this doesn't sound like a lack of faith resulting in a lack of healing. I would say, yes it does, in this case. **Therefore, we cannot say that lack of faith *never* results in continued sickness, poverty, or misery. But neither can we say that lack of faith always results in a lack of healing**; there are many counter examples that show people with little or no faith receiving a miracle.

I will not seek to be exhaustive in finding all such examples, but a few will suffice to make the point. Take

---

[22] (Fee 2006)

for example the healing of two men possessed by demons described in Matthew 8 (and a similar individual described in Mark 5 and Luke 8); it would seem that neither they nor anyone else would have given these men any hope of being healed. No one seems to be full of faith that Jesus will heal the men and yet they are healed just the same. In Luke 7 we read of a man who has died, and his friends and family are in the middle of a funeral procession when Jesus brings the man back to life. Certainly, the man in question could not have had faith in this miracle and neither do the crowd attending him seem to have any faith that a miracle is about to occur and yet an amazing miracle does occur and the crowd is astonished and fearful.

Allow me to draw our attention to one more example where lack of faith did not prevent a miracle. Turning to John 5, we read of a man who had been lame for 38 years. He has seen much in his time of sickness and it seems that his faith is at a very low ebb. When Jesus asks him if he wants to be healed, he is so lacking in faith that he actually tells Jesus that he cannot get well (John 5:6-7). Then Jesus heals him anyway.

So, what do we take away from all of this? We find that there are times when a lack of faith did appear to prevent miracles from happening and there are other occasions where a lack of faith was no barrier at all. We would do well to be very careful in how we counsel people about the reason why they did or did not receive a miracle, especially since telling someone that the reason they did not receive a miracle was because of their lack of faith would be terribly destructive. We must also be careful to recognize that Jesus says that our faith can be very powerful. He tells us that "faith as small as a mustard seed" will move mountains. Thus, it appears that we will have to leave some room for uncertainty. When we live by faith and ask the Lord to provide a miracle, we do not know what the answer will be. There are other factors beyond our faith or lack of faith that play a role in the answers we receive.

In the context of this discussion, I am reminded of further wise words from C.S. Lewis who is well-known for his words about Aslan in *The Lion, the Witch, and the Wardrobe*. There, in response to a question about the nature of the lion, Mr. Beaver responds, "Safe?...Who said anything about safe? 'Course he isn't safe. But he's good. He's the King, I tell you."[23] Of course these words of Lewis are theologically loaded and express his own opinion on the nature of Jesus. **He is telling us that no matter how much we study the person of Jesus, we will still find much mystery and unpredictability. Jesus is good, but he is not safe, predictable, or straightforward.** Therefore, we should be careful of what we do and don't expect from Jesus and we must be extremely careful as we counsel others about their understanding of faith, healings, and miracles.

---

[23] Lewis, C.S., 1950. *The Lion, the Witch, and the Wardrobe.* Samuel French Ltd.

> In the present discussion, a brief word regarding the view set forth in the Westminster Confession (1646) is in order. That particular document has this to say: God the great Creator of all things does uphold, direct, dispose, and govern all creatures, actions, and things, from the greatest even to the least, by his most wise and holy providence, according to his infallible foreknowledge, and the free and immutable counsel of his own will, to the praise of the glory of his wisdom, power, justice, goodness, and mercy.[24]

This is a statement of God's providence or common grace and suggests that God gives all people a level of care that is representative of his common grace toward us all. In some cases, this is what is behind the concept that "everything is a miracle," and indeed, God showers us with his miracles every day. Some would suggest that the everyday miracles of life are all that one can expect in these times. Some within the Reformed tradition (from which this confession originates) would allow for the supernatural that extends beyond common grace and others would be hesitant to speak of supernatural events occurring in this world. The

---

[24] Center for Reformed Theology and Apologetics, Westminster Confession, Chapter V, Section 1, https://reformed.org/documents/wcf_with_proofs/index.html?body=/documents/wcf_with_proofs/ch_V.html

Westminster Confession helps us to see the hand of God in all things, but it does not answer the fundamental questions we are seeking to answer in the present discussion.

Now it is time for me to "come clean," so to speak, and reveal my own position on the supernatural and miracles of God. The thesis I wish to put forward in this book is that the truth lies somewhere between the philosophy of Deism and the hyper-supernaturalism premise; between Cessationism that says we can no longer experience miracles and expecting a miracle at every turn. From my perspective, it appears that we live in a universe in which God has created a self-contained creation that, for the most part, functions in a cause-and-effect manner and does not require his intervention at every stage of the day. He sheds upon all his common grace, which includes the normal functions of biology, chemistry, and physics. He has embedded certain constants in our world that make it possible for us to live on this earth in our corner of the universe: the speed of light, the 23-degree tilt of the axis of our planet, the melting point, the density of water, and many other scientific constants. He also seems to reserve the right to enter into his creation at certain points in the story and to break into the normal structures and physics of the universe to do supernatural events.

When I speak of "my perspective," I mean by that, the perspective of a man who has followed Jesus since he was 15, has lived 58 years on this earth, and has experienced about five to ten incidents that I would say constitute miraculous events. What five to ten events? We shall talk more about these in subsequent chapters, but the specifics of the incidents that I would classify as miracles are less important than the fact that I am suggesting that I have witnessed, on average, one or two miracles per decade. That is significant and means that I have witnessed a world in which God is still working and doing things beyond the empirical systems of cause and effect, but not so often as to see the miraculous as the only, or majority, manner in which God works. That is the thesis that will guide the rest of this book and the reader must decide if I have made a sufficient case to convince them of the truth of this thesis.

But before we go on, I must also comment on the continued purpose of miracles. If I am suggesting that God still does perform miracles in our world today, why would he use them? There would need to be a reason. Why would God still do miracles in this era? The Cessationists might have a point that we have all of the evidence we need in the Canon of the Old and New Testaments of the Bible. Why do we need miracles today?

In answer to the why question, I will start with a quote from Tim Stafford, "Healing happened in Jesus' day as a foretaste of his resurrection. Healing happens today as a foretaste of *our* resurrection."[25] As C.S. Lewis has reminded us, God is always seeking to woo humans into relationship with him,[26] and so he seeks to remind us of the resurrection of Jesus and our future hope of resurrection. In fact, we might even go farther than this and say that miracles in the Old Testament of the Bible were also a foretaste. Old Testament miracles were prophecy that pointed ahead to the coming Messiah and to the incarnation of God as man in the form of Jesus. **Miracles have that effect on us: they point us back to what God has done in the past and ahead to what God will do in the future.** This is the reason God is still doing miracles. He is not doing them to prove his existence. I have previously suggested there could never be enough miracles to prove that God exists and that there would always be a way to explain them away. But miracles do point to the power of God and require us to consider the possibility of his existence. They point back to the resurrection and point forward to the ultimate return of Jesus at the end of the age. Miracles today are indeed a foretaste of the resurrection life we will one day experience.

In Luke 11:20, Jesus says, "… if I am casting out demons by the power of God, then the Kingdom of God has arrived among you." The broader context of that

---

[25] Stafford, Tim. 2012. Miracles. Bloomington: Bethany House Publishers.
[26] Lewis, C.S. *The Screwtape Letters*. New York: MacMillan Publishing Co., Inc, 1980, p. 38, 39.

passage shows that the miracles of Jesus were a sign that he had ultimate power over nature, pain, sickness, and the devil. So, while Jesus was on the earth, his miracles pointed to something greater than the physical world; they pointed to the rule of God over all of creation and anticipated the crowning miracle of all time – the resurrection. Jesus' miracles and his resurrection from the dead were signs that he had ultimate power over life and death.

Contemporary miracles that have occurred since the resurrection of Jesus similarly point to his final return to rule over all of creation. William Young, in a paper entitled "Miracles in Church History" puts it this way:

> We mistake when we treat the Spirit and his gifts as though we had the right to expect the full payment now, in this life. As Tom Smail puts it: Charismatics are constantly tempted to seek a costless triumph whereby they receive all the kingdoms of the world and their glory in an easier way than God's way, and so inevitably at another hand than God's hand.-' It is consonant with the conception of 'foretaste' that while some may be healed, not all are healed. It is fitting that we should find miracles in the course of Church history, but not fitting

that they should be happening all the time."[27]

It seems that Young would agree with me that miracles are still happening and yet he is also seeking to avoid the hyper-supernaturalism to which I have referred. He is saying that God's supernatural miracles in our day are merely a foretaste of the full expression of God's heavenly kingdom. We should not expect life to be too easy here on Earth, this side of the complete expression of the Kingdom of God. **The miracles we experience today are imperfect representations of a perfect future.**

A further reason for present day miracles is related to God's guidance in our lives. As we have said, it seems that God does not intervene supernaturally very often, but when he does, it is at times of people's greatest need. I spoke of my own healing miracle as a touchstone event in my life. It came at a particularly important time in my life because I had just left a good paying and stable job as a scientist in a molecular genetics lab to go and start new churches. Perhaps this incident was part of the way in which God chose to spur me on in my faith and encourage me in this new and less stable work. Similar to

---

[27] Paper by William Young, "Miracles in Church History" https://biblicalstudies.org.uk/pdf/churchman/102-02_102.pdf; see also T. Smail in Theological Renewal. No.8. p.4.

Gideon's experience,[28] God may intervene when a person has a particular need for guidance and needs a clear picture of God's will for their lives. Is this another example of how he continues to woo us into relationship with him and keep us on the path of his will for our lives?

Is this a reasonable approach? The reader will need to make their own assessment based on my argument here, what the individual has experienced in the world, and the tradition that has informed their understanding of the Bible and the supernatural. C.S. Lewis said that "the question of whether miracles occur can never simply be answered by experience,"[29] and I would agree. Lewis said that ultimately the question is a philosophical one and will be dependent upon the way in which we engage the world. Yet as a starting point, we need to hear of other people's experiences and begin to assess what we think may be happening in these events. To convince you of my humble thesis I need to begin by speaking of a few more miracles that I believe qualify as supernatural events. I will begin to do this in the next chapter.

---

[28] Judges 6:33-40
[29] (Lewis, Miracles 2015)

## Chapter 5: A Few Good Miracles

It was a Thursday night toward the end of a busy week, April 19, 2018. I had gone to bed early and slept well until 3:30am. Our youngest daughter, Lauren, was pregnant with her third child and was due to deliver in about six months. I dreamed that the phone rang and I answered it to the sounds of someone crying and in deep distress. In the dream, it was Lauren calling to tell us that she had had a miscarriage. She was inconsolable, and I too was deeply saddened. I soon awoke in a sweat with tears in my eyes, thankful that it had all been just a dream. However, I found that the dream had spoiled any possibility of sleeping at that moment and so I got up out of bed and found my way to the living room to pray. I prayed that God would not allow such a thing to happen and asked God to protect this pregnancy, this unborn child, and our daughter. After 15 minutes of pouring out my heart to God, I crept back into bed trying not to wake my wife and slept soundly until my alarm went off.

That morning, we received an actual telephone call from Lauren. She called to say that the night before she had begun to bleed and experience cramping. She was going to have to go in to see her doctor to figure out what was happening. I was shocked that my dream seemed so much like real life. I did not give her details at the time; I did not want to scare her any more than she already was.

Yet I did tell her that something had woken me in the night that caused me to spend some time praying for her. My wife and I continued to pray as we waited to hear the results of her consultation with her doctor. She got back to us later that day to say that the doctor thought that what she had experienced was a normal amount of spotting and that there did not seem to be any major concern. The doctor told her to take it easy for a few days and see how she felt. In the next few days, the spotting cleared up and we were all encouraged.

**I pondered these things in my heart and wondered about the timing of these events. Was this a miracle? Was it a coincidence that I woke in the middle of the night to pray for Lauren when she needed that type of prayer?** Today our daughter has a beautiful baby girl, safely delivered on November 4. This incident may seem like a small thing to many who hear it and I readily confess that it is impossible to prove that a miracle occurred.

In one sense it would be easier to say that my prayers were a coincidence and had no bearing on actual events. That would remove one puzzling and painful issue: why do some miscarriages still occur without the intervention of a dream and prayers of a father? Why would God give a miracle such as this to one person and not to another? If God woke me in the night to pray for the life of a baby, why doesn't he wake me up other nights for other pregnancies, or for people who might otherwise be hit by a drunk driver, or for any other myriad of things I ought to pray about? God could have me awake every night to pray for the struggles of our world. God could wake up thousands of individuals and whole church communities to pray for things that need to be prayed about. Why would he choose to wake me on this one night to pray? I almost want to say that this could not be a miracle because it is too painful to consider other situations where God does not intervene. Of course, in another sense, I want this whole experience to be a genuine miracle prompted by a dream that woke me in the night and the loving answers to prayer of an omnipotent God. What am I to believe?

These are the struggles inherent in the writing of a book such as this. I must tell my own story that is full of faith and doubts and continued questions about the way in which a loving God works in our world. I do find that incidents such as being wakened in the night to pray for something happen from time to time in my life. Am I simply more prone to this than some? Do these events happen to others who speak less of them? I ask the reader to consider their own experience in such things. Ought we see these as coincidences or divine intervention?

Over the last few months and years, I have been actively collecting stories from others who have experienced things that appear to be miraculous events. The rest of this chapter will give a short inventory of events that, as explained by witnesses, defy natural explanation and are strong candidates for supernatural occurrences. I have mostly used first-hand accounts where I have had opportunity to speak to the person who experienced the potentially miraculous event. Occasionally I have had to settle for well-researched second and third-hand accounts. Neither first-hand, second-hand, nor third-hand accounts will be irrefutable. I have already asserted that God will not give us irrefutable evidence. **I will tell the stories and leave it to the reader to assess the probability of the miraculous for each one.** You might like to develop your own system that assigns a score to each, or you may simply go with your gut feeling. But - I encourage us to notice that if even one of these events seems to be a miraculous event, we have grounds to have hope for a world that includes the supernatural and miraculous.

I recently had opportunity to travel to Cuba with a group of pastors from Canada and the United States. A pastor we met there leads a network of house churches and sports ministries in Cuba. We stayed in their primary facility that serves as a ministry centre, meeting area, church meeting place, and guest house. We travelled to surrounding towns to visit house churches. The ministry extends to 104 house churches in various places in Cuba, which I will not identify, for the house churches are part of an underground movement. In January of 1959, under the leadership of Che Guevara and Fidel Castro, the Communist Party of Cuba took power and began reconstructing the country and the constitution to make

Cuba an atheistic, communist, socialist country. Churches that existed in church buildings at the time were allowed to remain but strict guidelines on renovations and control of the congregations were put in place.

Today, in order to propagate the gospel in Cuba in places that do not have vital churches, the people of Cuba rely upon "underground" house churches. The authorities tolerate these house churches but are ever watchful to see that they do not become too popular. When we were in the country, we were taught to be very careful of who we photographed, and we were told not to put any pictures of events or people on social media because the government was watching. I preached at one house church filled to capacity with courageous Cuban people whose place of worship had been closed and torn down just a few months before. They had been meeting in a small shed in an alley next to several apartment blocks. A member of the Communist Party had started to attend the meeting and was turning toward Jesus. It may have been that the party member brought the meeting to the attention of the authorities. It may have been that the church just became too popular and was not hidden away inside an apartment, but one day the authorities came to the location, told people they could no longer meet there, and tore down the shed. Undeterred in their enthusiasm for Jesus, the people courageously began meeting in a nearby apartment owned by one of the women in the church. On the day I worshipped with them, they were playing a keyboard and singing joyful music that carried out into the streets. Although I preached through a translator, I was the one who went away encouraged and strengthened in my faith. I say all of this to alert us to the type of pressure placed upon Christians in this part of the world. They are constantly observed and discriminated against but press on with a simple faith in Jesus. A loving God who wanted to encourage these faithful followers could certainly use supernatural occurrences to strengthen their faith. While this team of North American leaders and I were in Cuba, we heard stories of miraculous events that had taken place in their midst.

One was a 22-year-old Christian who described herself as once being a "wild child" who drank excessively, went with several men, and was in a self-destructive mode. She had learned English and was hired by a pastor to do some translation work and, as a by-product, began to hear the Gospel. One night, while she was drunk, she had a vision of herself dying and having to pass through the cross of Jesus to get to "the other side." The vision scared her, and she investigated the claims of Christ and became a Christian. In the week we were there, she was translating for one of the pastors on our team as he preached in a house church. She gladly tells the story of her transformation as a description of how God miraculously intervened and drew her to a different path.

At this point, I will add in a third-hand miraculous experience so that we might demonstrate the way in which the Catholic Church comes to conclusions about supernatural events. As we have already said, the Vatican has a very strict process for how it investigates miracles. They spent 14 years analysing the case of a four-year-old Colorado Springs boy named Luke with a serious gastrointestinal condition. In 1998, doctors had tried antibiotics, diets, and extensive testing and still the boy was afflicted with eight to ten bouts of diarrhea per day that caused him to lose weight and get sicker and sicker. They did not know how to cure him. The boy's mother looked for help outside of medicine and asked a group of nuns to pray for her son. Sister Margaret Mary Preister and Sister Evangeline Spenner prayed to the German founder of their order, Mother Theresia Bonzel, who had lived approximately 100 years previous to their time. The nuns prayed in a nine-day vigil and asked Mother Theresia Bonzel to intervene and heal Luke. As soon as the nuns had finished their prayer vigil, the boy woke up without pain in his stomach and the illness never returned. The mother was certain it was a miracle, but the Vatican took 14 years to confirm that they also believed it to be a miracle.[30] Mother Theresia Bonzel's beatification process was begun in 1961 and was not completed until 2013.[31] The miracle of young Luke from Colorado Springs, USA

---

[30] Draper, Electa. "Vatican declares healing of Colorado Springs boy a miracle after prayers to German nun." *Denver Post*, April 30, 2016. See also
http://www.beliefnet.com/inspiration/7-modern-miracles-that-science-cant-explain.aspx?p=6

[31] Ibid

was a significant factor in the process. As I do not have first-hand knowledge of this miracle, I am limited by the articles I have read in trusted periodicals such as the Denver Post. The slow and careful process of the Catholic Church also gives me a sense of confidence that something miraculous happened here.

The life of James Smithman, with whom I have spoken, provides another example of events worthy of consideration as miraculous. James was told about Jesus from the time that he was born. His mother was a godly woman who attended a Presbyterian church in California. James reminds me that Presbyterian churches are not known for outbursts of charismatic activity and his mother's church was no exception. **Not many would expect a full-blown miracle to occur within the confines of their property or their theology.** James remembers many happy Sundays in the church building, but he also remembers a day when he was just plain bored. James was a few days short of his fifth birthday and had significant difficulty in hearing what was going on in church. Doctors had told his mother that James was going to need surgery to correct his near-deafness. James was small for his age, but his ear canals were particularly small. In fact, the doctors said that the canals were narrowing rather than growing, leading to ever poorer hearing. The surgery would be necessary to correct the problem before his hearing was permanently lost.

James says that on this particular day in church, he must have been fidgeting, or rustling some papers, or making noise because his mother turned to him and said, "James, settle down. Why don't you just sit there and pray that God would heal your hearing so that you don't need surgery?" The mother knew that there were costs involved in surgery, and James wasn't keen on having to go to the hospital for the surgery either. So when his mother told him to pray for healing, James thought, "Okay, that would be a good idea," and he pulled out the kneeling bench while the preacher preached and James got down on his knees and prayed as only an almost five-year-old could pray.

**Immediately James heard a pop, like pressure in his ears had been released. Then came a rumble of popping sounds in his ears.** Forty years later, James says, it felt like his ears "blew open." He turned and looked at his mother and said, "Mom, why is the man yelling?" His mother returned a quizzical look and he asked the same question again, "Why is that man so loud?" Mother and son realized that James was now hearing clearly the voice of the preacher. Compared to what James *had been* hearing, the voice sounded very loud. That's when James and his mother realized he had been healed. Shortly after the healing, his mother took him back to the doctors who confirmed that the ear canals were no longer too small for the boy. They had quickly grown to an appropriate size. Now, forty-plus years later, James' hearing is better than average, and he praises God that he received a supernatural healing at five years of age.

James readily recognizes that it is natural for ear canals to grow and it could be expected that his might have grown to the appropriate size. He believes what sets this experience apart and puts it in the realm of the supernatural is the timing of how his ear canals grew to the right size just at the time when he prayed for healing, and when he prayed that he might not require surgery. Could this have happened spontaneously at that time without prayer? That's a possibility. But today, James speaks of this miracle as a touchstone event in his life. It is a moment in time that has shaped the rest of his life. **Whenever he finds himself questioning the power of God, whenever he wonders whether his faith is real, whenever he questions whether or not God even exists, he remembers that moment in time and finds grounding in his spiritual life. Isn't that just the kind of reason God might provide a miracle?** Isn't that just the kind of encouragement God might give a man to guide him through the rest of his life?

Let's take a look at a situation in which the miracles are more difficult to see. As I write this book, our church has been praying for a man (we will call him Adam), his wife, and their young daughter. Adam went to his doctor for a regular check-up and the doctor drew some blood and did some tests. Something showed up that did not appear normal and they ordered more tests and imaging. When the results were available the doctors concluded that Adam had Pancreatic Neuroendocrine Tumours (PNETS) with metastatic tumours in the liver. A large tumour in the pancreas was beginning to undergo a process of encasement, indicating that it had been there for a while. Approximately three other significant tumours were present in the liver, ranging in size from golf-ball size to the size of a lime. Some of his doctors saw this as ominous and wondered if he would live through the next few months.

Soon after they received the news, Adam and his wife called the church and asked if someone could pray with them. I went to their home, prayed, and anointed him with oil. The elders of our church did the same a few days later. The couple showed a great deal of confidence in Jesus and trusted him to bring healing to Adam's life. All of us asked Jesus to take away this cancer and remove the tumours from his body. Adam and his wife, in their own words, "leaned into Jesus" and spent much time listening to worship music, reading the Bible, and praying together. They, the elders, and I, asked Jesus to bring them healing, peace, and joy in the midst of the struggle. Adam still felt well and could not even tell that he was sick without the evidence of the tests and x-rays. We prayed that the next time Adam went to the doctor they would find he was completely free of tumours and cancer. But when next he went to the doctors the tumours were still there and the diagnosis of cancer was still given. Our Lord had said "no" to the particular type of supernatural event for which we had hoped.

Yet there were everyday miracles in the life of Adam. The fact that this couple were drawn closer to Jesus through this process is somewhat supernatural in itself. Many young men with young families would have been likely to curse God and become bitter. Adam and Linda did just the opposite. They called upon God and drew closer to him. The fact that this cancer was discovered before Adam felt any symptoms was surprising and potentially miraculous. The fact that he felt so well and stayed healthy for so long was quite possibly supernatural. Yet *these* miracles would be hard for any of us to see. On the surface they look like nothing at all.

Then came a time in which we waited. The doctors recommended that no treatment would be initiated at this time, and they would reassess after Adam's body had a chance to fight this cancer. For three months this couple waited, while praying, listening to worship music, praising God, and reading the Bible. When they returned for the next series of tests, everyone was surprised to find that the tumours had not grown. Despite a diagnosis of cancer, there was no appreciable change in his health. The doctors again recommended that no treatment be initiated, and another three-month period be allowed to pass before reassessment. As I write these words we are still praying for Adam, Linda, and their daughter, and we wait to see what else the Lord might do in this situation. It is an unfinished story and yet this couple has said that they feel that their faith has been strengthened even more than if God had miraculously taken away the tumours after the first period of prayer. The stability of Adam's health coupled with the fact that he still has the disease has caused them to keep on trusting in God who continues to hold them in his hand.

Another miracle story comes to us from Tim Stafford, a journalist for *Christianity Today* who speaks of his friend Jeff and says:

> … a young man in my church, had fully expected to spend his life in a wheelchair. Years of multiple surgeries had done nothing for him, and one of the top specialists in the country had told him to stop hoping for a cure and accept the excruciating pain as it was. Then, at the invitation of a friend, he rolled his wheelchair into a Pentecostal church one Sunday morning. He walked out pain-free. That was four years ago. He has never felt pain in his feet since. At a word of prayer, he was completely, instantly healed.[32]

---

[32] https://www.christianitytoday.com/ct/2012/september/a-new-age-of-miracles.html

Stafford goes on to tell how he spent a significant amount of time investigating this apparent miracle. He spoke with the young man and with witnesses to the healing. He interviewed others who had prayed for healing at the same Pentecostal church. He spoke with those who had not received healing and those who had. Although I have never met Stafford, and his story is not first-hand to me, it has additional credibility because he works for a respected journal and book publisher, both of whom wish to continue their reputation of responsible journalism.[33] In a world of controversy over "fake news," opinion has taken a toll on responsible journalism. We find ourselves asking questions about how we can trust reporting in any of its forms. Yet the standards remain the same as they were years ago before the proliferation of web-based news. We find sources we can trust. We look to periodicals and publishers who have consistently told us the truth and we carefully read what they present, looking for any signs of bias.

In this case, we have Stafford's reputation in other articles he has written, the methodology of the writer as he carefully investigated the events, Stafford's rational skepticism that he brings to bear on the events he is investigating, and the reputation of the publisher. All of this gives us greater trust in the conclusions of Stafford in this regard. **Again, each reader will need to use their own criteria as they come to conclusions about the**

---

[33] (Stafford 2012)

**supernatural, but certainly it must be a logical and faith-filled process.** As I write this book, I am also hopeful that the volume of evidence that is being accumulated may help the reader as they consider their approach to the miracles of God.

I will close this chapter with one more miracle story. I have previously referred to the time in which doctors identified a mass on the pons of my brain (chapter three), which was also the same time when I spent many years praying for my friend Jason who eventually died from the ravages of multiple myeloma. What I have not yet related is the events that were happening at the same time in the life of my wife, Maureen. Maureen's father had died due to the complications of early-onset Parkinson's Disease. His symptoms began to occur in his early 40's and he died at the relatively young age of 58. Not all forms of Parkinson's Disease are hereditary but some of the early onset forms are heritable. Consequently, when Maureen, in her early 40's, noticed that she was developing tremors, she began to investigate. She was referred to a neurologist who performed a number of tests designed to rule out other neurological causes for the tremor and confirmed our worst fears: the doctor believed that Maureen had a form of early onset Parkinson's. The neurologist began to follow her progress, anticipating that her symptoms would become progressively worse. When this neurologist was no longer available, Maureen began seeing another neurologist who again examined Maureen and concurred with the diagnosis of early-onset Parkinson's.

As you may recall from Chapter Three, at this time, two friends and I spent one hour every Wednesday afternoon praying for various needs, including Jason's cancer, the mass on my pons, and now Maureen's diagnosis of Parkinson's Disease. For Maureen, we prayed specifically that she would either be completely healed of this disease or that the symptoms would progress so slowly that it would not be a major burden on her life. One of the hallmarks of early-onset Parkinson's is the fact that it continues to progress quickly. Maureen's father was in a wheelchair by the time he was 56. So, looking at the family history, the doctors anticipated that Maureen's progression might be similar. But, in this case, three friends were praying every week for about seven or eight years for Maureen's health. During those years, Maureen's symptoms were still there but they progressed at a slow pace.

In 2008 when Maureen was 48, we moved to Vancouver, British Columbia. She found that over the next six months, her tremors began to diminish. The move to a different city necessitated a change of doctors and a new round of testing with a neurologist in Vancouver. Maureen went through the usual battery of tests designed to distinguish Parkinson's from any other neurological disorders. Doctors examined how she walked, the movement of her hands, her smile and facial expressions, and a few other clinical traits. The conclusion was surprising. The doctor now found no evidence that she had Parkinson's. Yes, there seemed to be a small tremor, but that was all that was left from the previous diagnosis of Parkinson's.

This one still leaves both Maureen and me scratching our heads today. **Did the doctors in Calgary simply make a wrong diagnosis? Such things have been known to happen. Or did several years of faithful prayer make a difference and a slow healing? We will never know.** I tend to lean toward a belief in a healing miracle. I think Maureen is less certain of this. This story is ambiguous enough to leave it solidly in the realm of mystery. Certainly, that is how God works in this world and so we leave it in his hands. Maybe one day we will have a chance to know the answer directly from him.

Looking to a fuller expression of an excerpt from C.S. Lewis' book *Miracles*, we are again reminded of what is at stake. Listen as he summarises the relationship between experience and philosophy:

> "For this reason, the question whether miracles occur can never be answered simply by experience. Every event that might claim to be a miracle is, in the last resort, something presented to our senses, something seen, heard, touched, smelled or tasted. And our senses are not infallible. If anything extraordinary seems to have happened, we can always say that we have been the victims of an

> illusion. If we hold a philosophy that excludes the supernatural, this is what we always shall say. What we learn from experience depends on the kind of philosophy we bring to experience. It is therefore useless to appeal to experience before we have settled, as well as we can, the philosophical question."[34]

By now, we have spoken of a number of incidents that may be considered miracles or may be written off as illusions. Lewis and I are very much aware that we cannot settle the issues by shouting a little louder and finding a few more events that look like supernatural in-breakings of God. At the end of the day, what will settle the matter for each of us will be the philosophical bent with which we come to the subject. Yet, for me, **I find that hearing what has happened in the life of others is a starting point, a place to begin to consider how I will settle the philosophical question.** Perhaps we have a "chicken and egg" question here. Which comes first, settling our philosophy of miracles and allowing experience to provide evidence for our position, or allowing experiences to point us toward a settling of the philosophical question? I suspect that it is a mix of the two and that both philosophy and experience must work together.

---

[34] (Lewis, Miracles 2015)

## Chapter 6: Good News to the Celts

We pulled up at the green and aged wrought iron gates a little after 9:00 am and were sad to see they were locked. We shrugged and thought we would have to miss out on this sight-seeing event in Ireland. Driving back up the road less than a kilometre to the village of Durrow, we walked through the beautiful cemetery associated with the church there. A little more online research about the place we had been trying to see and my wife found a phone number for someone who might know about the site. A very friendly woman said, "Oh, is the gate not yet open? It is supposed to be open by now. I will make a call and call you back." Five minutes later she was back on the line with my wife. "It should be open any minute." We thanked her and headed back to the gates. A few minutes after we arrived, a pick-up truck pulled up from inside the gates and opened them for our entrance.

Thus, we were welcomed into one of the most ancient Christian sites in all of Ireland: the Durrow Chapel and Abbey. The site is now owned by the Irish National Trust and they intend to turn it into a tourist attraction, but not until they have built a better road than the present dirt trail. So, to our good fortune, we had the place to ourselves that morning. We poked around the gravestones in the ancient cemetery and explored the low rock wall around the cemetery. Some of the crumbling structures we saw had been there since 550 CE[35] when the abbey had first been established. The church on the site was built in the 18th or 19th century on the footprint of at least one other church that dates back to around 1100 CE. It strikes awe in one's heart to see this eight-foot high cross with more than a dozen carvings depicting various biblical stories. It too dated back to the twelfth century or earlier.

But we saved the best for last. Walking just a little further north and east, we found the ancient well that had been there since before the original abbey was established by Columcille in 550 CE (the well may be as old as 350 CE). The well has been used ever since the chapel was established, both for common use and for holy water in religious services. You can still crouch down and get to the water of the well and so we had a marvelous spiritual time as we touched the water and used it to make the sign of the cross on ourselves, even as so many who had gone before had done. We basked in the knowledge that great and fearless missionaries of the faith had walked in this place and planted walnut and apple trees whose genetic descendants still grew on this land and we expressed our gratitude to those who had kept the faith alive in that place just 500 years after the resurrection of Jesus. We praised God for how he has sustained his church these many years

---

[35] Throughout this book I will use CE to designate Common Era. This is the same as the older reference, AD: Anno Domini. The other designation of BCE (Before the Common Era will also be used) rather than BC (Before Christ).

since the Christians who had been on this property had had a vibrant community life in Durrow.

Columcille, who established the religious community whose ruins we had just explored, was an Irish monk also known as St. Columba. He is and was a great hero of the Celtic Christian faith, an Irish Abbot, and missionary evangelist who trained at the Clonard monastic school and established the Durrow Abbey before spending much of his life establishing churches, abbeys, and monasteries in Scotland. The ruins we had visited were just the beginning for this bold servant of Jesus Christ.

The heritage of Columba and the Durrow community of faith dates back a century before Columba to Patricius (later known as Saint Patrick), who had endured much hardship and danger as he brought the Good News of Jesus to much of Ireland. Patrick (or Patricius), who lived from 385 to 431 CE, lived too early to meet with Columba, but Patrick had an enormous influence on the monastic schools of Ireland. Like Paul the Apostle, Patrick was a Roman citizen. He lived in Roman-controlled Britain (perhaps what is now Scotland) but was taken as a slave by an Irish raiding party. In those days, it was common for a few fierce warriors to cross the Irish Sea and take people to tend their sheep or pigs in the hills. Patrick endured this cruel life for six years, always cold, and always hungry, before miraculously escaping. One night while he slept, a voice said to him, "Your hungers are rewarded: you are going home. Look, your ship is ready."[36] Immediately, Patrick set out across country to find a port, a distance of 200 miles. After initially being turned away, he was welcomed on board a cargo ship and eventually landed in Britain at a desolate part of the coast, where Patrick and the crew marched inland. Overcome with hunger, the captain of the ship taunted Patrick and asked him where his God was. Patrick responded with these words, "From the bottom of your heart, turn trustingly to the Lord my God, for nothing is impossible to him and today he will send you food for your journey until you are filled, for he has abundance everywhere." Patrick and the crew then knelt and prayed this prayer. As they rose, a herd of wild pigs stampeded toward them and they were able to kill some and have a great feast.

**Upon his return to Britain, Patrick thought much about the Irish need of the Gospel.** He kept

---

[36] Sources of research for this chapter include Cahill's work, *How The Irish Saved Civilization, Life of St. Columba* by Adomnan, and Wikipedia. Each of these publications contain many of the same facts and when I am not using direct quotes it is difficult to say where I may have gathered the information. Many of the stories of the lives of Patrick and Columba have come to be part of the public record. I will not reference every thought that may have come from one of these sources but I am indebted to them nonetheless. Cahill's work is certainly a good source and contains a good deal of the history of Celtic Christianity for those who would like more history than I am sharing in this book.

hearing their cries as they asked for help, in both his dreams and his waking moments. He eventually returned and had great success in sharing the message of Jesus with the Irish people. Thomas Cahill, in the book, *How the Irish Saved Civilization*, writes:

> With the Irish—even with the kings—he succeeded beyond measure. Within his lifetime or soon after his death, the Irish slave trade came to a halt, and other forms of violence, such as murder, and intertribal warfare, decreased. In reforming Irish sexual mores, he was rather less successful, though he established indigenous monasteries and convents, whose inmates by their way of life reminded the Irish that the virtues of lifelong faithfulness, courage, and generosity were actually attainable by ordinary human beings and that the sword was not the only instrument for structuring a society.... Patrick is beyond dispute: the first human being in the history of the world to speak out unequivocally against slavery. Nor will any voice as strong as his be heard again until the seventeenth century.[37]

---

[37] Cahill, Thomas. *How the Irish Saved Civilization: The Untold Story of Ireland's Heroic Role from the Fall of Rome to the Rise of*

## Supernatural

Patricius, against all odds, became a holy man, a missionary, an evangelist, and an apostle to the Irish. Did he have divine guidance? Why would a man who had endured six years of slavery, cold, and hunger, later feel compassion toward his captures and return to that country? Might he not be enslaved once again? Might he not be forgiven if he feared these fierce and wild people of Ireland? It would have taken a clear call from God to leave the safety he had found and return to the land of his enslavement. It would indeed seem that God spoke to him through dreams, through his conscious thought processes, and through miracles of protection. After 1500 years it is difficult to distinguish miracle from myth, but there is certainly evidence that something beyond natural events and the ordinary actions of men and women were at work in the circumstances of Patrick's life. The speed with which the message of Christianity spread suggests that people were talking and even gossiping about something. Could it be that they could not stop speaking of the miracles worked by Patrick and his fellow missionaries? Could it be that God had done a miracle in the life of this once fearful slave and gave him the courage to be one of the greatest missionaries of all time?

Columba, whom we have already mentioned was another great missionary and who was inspired by and

---

*Medieval Europe.* New York: Anchor Books, A Division of Random House, Inc., 1995, p. 110.

followed in the spiritual footsteps of Saint Patrick. And so, in 563, Columba travelled to Kintyre Peninsula in Scotland with 12 companions (an intentional number) before settling at Iona and establishing a centre of literacy. He and his companions went on to found many more abbeys, chapels, monasteries, and churches all over Scotland. **What is most fascinating about the work of Saint Columba is that, like Patrick, and according to his biographers, everywhere he went his work was accompanied by signs and wonders.** There are many supernatural miracles associated with Columba's evangelistic missions and they are worthy of our analysis in the context of this discussion. Now of course, events that happened in the 6th century with accounts written years later are naturally hard to confirm and the writing style of authors who told the stories at that time were more concerned with confirming that the saint was a great leader than they were with historical accuracy. **Still, if we look at how quickly the gospel spread among the ancient people that were living in Scotland at the time, it suggests that something unusual was happening.** At the time, the people of Scotland consisted of the Picts, the Scots of Dál Riata, the Britons of Alt Clut, and the Anglian kingdom of Bernicia.[38] If we take the Picts as an example, we will readily see that these people were fierce and not easily swayed to a new way of life. Yet Columba and other Celtic missionaries evangelised these people, and did so in a relatively short period of time.

---

[38] (Wikipedia 2018)

The Pict people were so named due to their body paints which they wore into battle. In fact, they wore nothing else into battle. Their nakedness was a form of psychological warfare to intimidate their enemies. Furthermore, warriors who had decapitated an enemy in combat wore a torq (a stiff metal necklace) around their necks to indicate their warrior prowess to their enemies. As they went into battle, they screamed with great ferocity and contorted their faces to the extent that their enemies readily thought that they were demon possessed. These were the people to whom Columba went, without weapons or shields, to speak to them of the gospel of Jesus. Columba not only survived his interactions with these people, he and his companions were able to make a radical change in the culture of these people in just a few years. What was behind this rapid transformation of culture?

One story, recounted in Adamnan's *Life of St. Columba*, shows the boldness with which Columba entered into his mission and the confidence he had in God to protect him. Columba and his companions had come into a new region under the rule of the Pict king, Bridei (also sometimes written as Brude), who had a fortress at Fortriu. We are told that Bridei, full of pride and self-confidence, would not open the gates of his fortress to Columba's group. Columba, seeing that the gate was not open to him, appealed to God to open it by making the sign of the cross on the door. Immediately the bolt was driven back with great force and the gate opened by itself. Columba and his companions entered the fortress and began to make their way to the king. King Bridei, hearing what had happened, was filled with fear and showed Columba great respect, allowing him to present the gospel in Bridei's kingdom. What might this encounter have looked like if God had not intervened on behalf of Columba? How much does a simple miracle of this nature enhance the progress of the mission of God in this new territory for the gospel? **If miracles like this were happening, it would certainly explain why these fierce warriors took notice of these strange missionaries in their midst.**

Adamnan relates many more such supernatural events in the life of Columba. There are miracles in which people are rescued from storms and dangerous animals, poisonous water is made safe, and even an incident where a dead person is brought back to life. Stories such as these, although difficult to confirm, do make sense of the rapid spread of the gospel throughout Scotland. If there is some truth to the many miracles attributed to Saint Columba, then the gospel spread, at least in part, as a result of supernatural events.

Thomas Cahill, in the previously mentioned book, puts less emphasis upon the miraculous events in the life of Columcille but still sees the rapid spread of the Gospel in Scotland as the providence of God. He relates that while Columcille was in Iona, he:

> ...began to dream of opening new monasteries. Among the rugged Scots and the scary Picts, especially Columcille's reputation spread like wildfire. (There wasn't after all, that much going on up that way.) He made one hundred fifty monks the cut off number for the Iona community, and after they had exceeded that, twelve and one monks would set off to establish another foundation in a new setting. Fresh applicants kept arriving in droves. By the time of Columcille's death in the last days of the sixth century, sixty monastic communities had been founded in his name along the jagged inlets and mountain heights of windswept Scotland.[39]

Every one of these sixty monastic communities made it a point to study and copy the great written works of the church. "Wherever they went they brought their love of learning and their skills in bookmaking. In the bays and valleys of their exile, they re-established literacy and breathed new life into the exhausted culture of Europe."[40] As Rome and much of Europe burned or had been

---

[39] Cahill. *How The Irish Saved Civilization*. 184, 185.
[40] Cahill, Thomas. *How The Irish Saved Civilization*. 196.

burned, and as the great libraries of the European world were destroyed by the Visgoths, Vandals, and other peoples, by God's grace and by God's supernatural, historical, intervention, the Irish monks faithfully copied every parchment, manuscript, and letter they could find. In the great monastic community at Iona and in smaller communities like the Durrow Abbey, the monks worked to preserve the great documents of their faith and the intellectual parchments of learning. Ireland's most famous manuscript, the beautiful Book of Kells, is believed to have been stored at Durrow to protect it from destruction. In Cahill's opinion, such protection actually saved civilization.

Similarly, by God's grace and through God's supernatural power, the Irish had been redeemed. In what we now call Scotland, the fierce warrior tribes were transformed by Patrick's spiritual disciple, Columcille. In the darkest of times, when the light of civilization was in danger of being snuffed out; in difficult and violent times, the mission of God continued throughout the world. Does it not seem plausible that God's supernatural power was at work, helping to spur God's people to greater accomplishments? Would others notice and tell the stories? I leave the reader to draw their own conclusions, but if we conclude that it was not because of supernatural influences that Christianity spread so rapidly, we must come up with other plausible sociological explanations for the transformation and those may be hard to find.

**Historical records of times and locations in which Christianity spread rapidly are full of stories of the supernatural, of prophetic visions, miraculous healings, and divine callings.** Time and space do not allow a full historical analysis, but history would suggest that there was supernatural involvement in the rapid spread of Christianity from 100 CE to 1200 CE in much of the known world of that time and many historians accommodate this explanation in the chain of events. We now turn to the *interaction* between natural and supernatural events in the next chapter.

## Chapter 7: On Science and the Supernatural

**I have often said that I fell in love with science before I fell in love with God.** From a very young age, I was a student of the sciences because after all, at its very roots, science is observation. Growing up on a farm in Central Alberta, there was plenty of time to observe the changes of the seasons, the growth of crops in the garden and the fields, the fecundity of rabbits, sheep, cattle, pigs, cats, and every wild animal known to that part of the world. On a mixed farm with everything from milk cows to oats, from sows to canola, from muskrat pelts to hay, and beef to peas, we soon learned which were the best producers and best crops so that we might be able to survive from the fruits of the land. The margins were narrow and being a keen observer of how things grew could mean the difference between a root cellar that lasted until next harvest time or not having sufficient food to get us through a long, snowy winter. We learned when to watch for wild berries and we canned and froze and cooked anything tasty and nutritious that might provide us with more food and less need to purchase things at the local stores. We butchered our own chickens and beef, we learned how to feed a steer to the proper size for good flavour and marbling of fat. We observed the flocking of crows, robins, and flickers as they prepared for their migrations and we watched carefully when they returned. Watching for signs of winter in the sky, vegetation, trees, and wild animals, we tried to beat nature at the game of life and death. The stars, sun, moon, and planets were mostly just there, but we also watched them to know how the seasons were advancing.

In about the third grade I discovered books. I became ravenous to learn all I could and was the guy who kept school librarians happy as I signed out the obscure books that no one else read. As time went on, I began to observe other things that piqued my interest in science: the marvel of photosynthesis, fairy rings in the lawn that indicated mycelial fungal structures, and a thousand other things. As I grew in age and knowledge, I took out more and more books on consistently more complicated topics. I found books on the flora and fauna of Alberta, biochemical reactions, genetics, and one of my favourites, a small volume on the mathematical formulas of Einsteinian physics. With a little help from an understanding teacher, I was able to work from the observations of Einstein through the math equations that led to his famous $E=mc^2$; an accomplishment I am not sure I could replicate today. But at the time, I saw the implications of how if one could travel at speeds very close to the speed of light, one would experience the dilation of time such that time would be experienced differently by subject and observer. I was awestruck by science and made it my objective to learn as much science as I could. I learned how to determine the direction of rotation of the moon around the earth by observation alone and learned about communal organisms such as bees and ants and observed their community "ethics" and division of labour. Years later I would write blog posts about tidal pools in the Pacific Ocean and how crows have learned to "do math" and recognize human faces. My love for science was set many years before I became a Christian at 15 years of age.

**When I did become a Christian, I discovered another affection: theology. After all, theology is simply the study of and love for God.** I memorized Bible verses and played Bible trivia with people in the church and soon found that I could hold my own with the elders and leaders of the church. I learned about theories of atonement and why the crucifixion of Jesus had greater depth than I could see on the surface. I studied the Psalms and saw great beauty; I studied Genesis and saw how God loved his creation. I found myself studying both science and theology and finding nothing in conflict. Contrary to what others might have experienced, I found nothing in the Bible that contradicted science and nothing in science that contradicted the Bible. I took at face value what the Bible said about God creating everything. I took at face value what scientists and science itself were saying about evolution and was able to meld them together in my own mind. It was not until several years later that I understood how some might see contradiction between the two. By that time, I had allies in people like Francis S. Collins, N.T. Wright, Dennis Venema, Kathryn Applegate, Scott McKnight, James K.A. Smith, and William T. Cavanaugh, who helped me develop a consistent understanding of God's creation and the Bible.

**So, when I speak of my commitment to miracles and the supernatural, I am at one and the same time committed to medicine, physics, chemistry, biology, engineering, and science in all of her forms.** I have not separated the world's knowledge into two parts: science and theology, but rather blended them together as one area of study. To use a line that many have used before me, "all truth is God's truth."[41] God's truth includes the relative invulnerability of the Tardigrade, or Water Bear (a creature that looks like it has stepped straight out of a sci-fi movie); it includes the fact that light travels at 299,792,458 metres per second; it includes the fact that the New Caledonian Crow can manufacture and use tools; it includes the truth that angels are messengers sent from God to communicate with his creation in general and to humans specifically; and it includes the truth that Jesus died a cruel death on a cross and triumphed over death by coming back to life. All of this and much more is the truth of God.

For 13 years I was employed as a Lab Scientist in the Molecular Diagnostic Lab of the Alberta Children's

---

[41] Attributed to many writers but likely has its roots in something Augustine (354-430 CE) said in one of his Latin works. "Nay, but let every good and true Christian understand that wherever truth may be found, it belongs to his Master…" *On Christian Doctrine* II.18.

Hospital in Calgary. When I was in the lab, I trusted that mixing Taq DNA polymerase, primer DNA, target DNA, and appropriate buffers while repeatedly heating and cooling the reaction would result in creating more of the target DNA. That series of chemical processes is what we call a polymerase chain reaction, or PCR. If it failed, I did not suspect that God had stopped my reaction from working; I assumed I had done something wrong that prevented the reaction from progressing. Similarly, I did expect the PCR would produce more of my target DNA and would not result in the production of a straw hat. If it did produce a straw hat, that would be magic or some kind of miracle, but no one would expect it and the God who allowed such chaos to occur would be some sort of trickster God like Loki of Norse mythology. I had to be able to trust that my reaction would amplify the DNA it targeted. I couldn't wonder if cause and effect would work one day but not the next. Science works. Cause and effect work because God created a universe in which cause and effect are the means whereby things happen. If a ball flies toward my house and breaks my window, I do not assume that the ball has always been in motion or that it picked itself up and hurled itself at my window. No, instead I go outside and look for the person who threw the ball through my window. God has made the universe to work this way unless he steps in and does something different. We can trust this to go on happening and we can trust that it has been happening for many centuries.

If I see light from a star and calculate that it has been travelling from the tremendous distance of $1.26 \times 10^{23}$ kilometres beyond earth, I know that the light from that star has been travelling for 13.3 billion years before reaching my eye. Of course, God could have done something miraculous and caused light to be created partway along the path toward my eye but, taken at face value, we would say that the light has travelled for 13.3 billion years. Nothing supernatural is required. Thus, our universe is this mix of natural and supernatural events with a heavy imbalance toward natural rather than supernatural events. If it were imbalanced toward the supernatural, we would see more supernatural events than natural events and we would never know what would happen each day as we went about our business. We might drive down the road and suddenly a rock would appear in the middle of the road or we might pour milk on our cereal and a rabbit would jump out of the bowl. Such a world would be chaotic and would not be suitable for human life. We trust that we live in a mostly natural world of cause and effect, action and reaction, not a supernatural world of magic.

So, as I learned from a young age, and many others have learned before, when one goes about investigating events that have a supernatural quality, it is perfectly reasonable to look at them with logic, science, and every faculty of the mind. Indeed, there are whole journal articles devoted to the scientific analysis of prayers that resulted in healing,[42] and this is a profitable way in which to investigate the supernatural. **If God gave us the ability to think with logic, why would he ask us to suspend this part of our mind when we enter the realm of miracles and the supernatural?**

Even as we say this and learn to investigate the miraculous with the rigor of logic and science, we must also make note of the limitations of each discipline of science and theology. Science is a very good tool. With it we have been able to improve medical interventions, develop immunizations that save lives around the world, invent satellite technologies that allow us to use global positioning systems (GPS) to find our way to the grocery store in another city, and create airplanes that get us safely around the world. Science is very good at investigating the world and answering questions like, "What are stars? How big is an onion cell? How many chromosomes are in the nuclei of a horse skin cell? How many are in a donkey? And how many in a mule?" With science we can investigate why a horse and a donkey can breed to produce a mule and we can see what this has to say about our own human chromosomes and what happens when such things as Trisomy 21 (also known as Down Syndrome) occur. Science is not good at answering questions like, "What was here before the universe? What is the purpose of life? Why are we humans here? And why is there something rather than nothing?"

---

[42] (Romez, Zaritzky and Brown 2019)

**So, the Bible doesn't tell us about horse chromosomes and science can't answer ultimate questions of life. These, it would seem, are the limits of each of these disciplines.** These are boundaries beyond which neither can pass. Yet, together, the two disciplines have much to say about this natural and supernatural world in which we live. Some have explained this by saying that God has given two books for us to read: the book of nature and the book of revelation. Nature, with the help of observation, science, and logic has much to say about the "what" of creation. Revelation in the inspired book of the Bible has much to say about the "why" of creation.

Galileo believed in reading these two books of God as long ago as 1615 CE when he wrote his "Letter to the Grand Duchess Christina." Galileo argued that God had written two books — the Book of Nature and the Book of Scripture. It was his opinion that these two books would not contradict one another. Years earlier, Augustine, in *The City of God*, wrote:

> Some people, in order to discover God, read books. But there is a great book: the very appearance of created things. Look above you! Look below you! Read it. God, whom you want to discover, never wrote that book with ink. Instead, He set before your eyes the things that He had

made. Can you ask for a louder voice than that?[43]

Of course, Augustine also believed God communicated through the Scriptures, but here he makes his point that the Bible is not God's only book.

There is another, lesser known individual who also demonstrates the fact that God communicates to us through the book of nature and the book of scripture. In 1927, a Jesuit Priest by the name of Georges Lemaître used his considerable research into theoretical physics and published a paper that was quite novel at the time. In this paper, he proposed that the universe had a beginning and that the beginning of the universe was an infinitely small point, a primeval atom, or a Cosmic Egg. This primeval atom then went on to expand into the tremendously large universe we have today. This concept of a universe with a beginning that started infinitely small and over time became very large is the same concept we now label the Big Bang Theory. Lemaître, a contemporary of Albert Einstein, sometimes lectured on the same circuits as Einstein and remained a faithful Jesuit priest even as he carried out significant teaching and research in theoretical physics. Lemaître believed in a Creator-God who shaped the universe in a logical structure that could be investigated by math and physics. **His faith in Jesus and**

---

[43] Augustine, "de Civitate Dei (City of God) book 16 (written 413-426 CE).

**his understanding of nature went hand in hand. For him there was no contradiction between faith and science, or miracles and nature.**

Looking back on some of what Lemaître said shows the significant blend of logical science, logical faith, and the mystery of creation. When he first explained his idea, Lemaître had this to say:

> If we go back in the course of time we must find fewer and fewer quanta, until we find all the energy of the universe packed in a few or even in a unique quantum [...] If the world has begun with a single quantum, the notions of space and time would altogether fail to have any meaning at the beginning; [...] we could conceive the beginning of the universe in the form of a unique atom, the atomic weight of which is the total mass of the universe.[44]

Allow me to emphasise that last sentence, "a unique atom, the atomic weight of which is the total mass of the universe." The statement is perfectly scientific and yet perfectly mysterious and maybe even philosophical and theological. He went on to speculate on how such

---

[44] Lemaître, G. (1931). The Beginning of the World from the Point of View of Quantum Theory. Nature 127: 706.

information might affect the Christian who pauses to think about such things. Being a person of faith himself he went on to speak of an intelligent being behind this "unique atom" and that our human minds could only begin to grasp the mystery of an atom with the atomic weight of the universe. He was most certainly a man of great faith and great science.

John Ortberg, Pastor at Menlo Church in Menlo Park, California had this to say about science and faith: "Jesus said that we are to love the Lord our God with all our mind. That means scientific investigation ought to be an act of worship.... And an enormously important endeavor for the church in our day...." He is advocating for an understanding of science and the supernatural that fit closely together. I am hopeful that this book might do the same.

I am convinced that we can allow science and faith to live side by side in this world. **The fact that I have studied both theology and science and have worked in both fields is often a surprise to people, but I would suggest that it should not be such a surprise.** When they hear that I went from being a lab scientist to a pastor they will often say, "That's quite a switch!" But why should that be a surprising thing? If God created a world that obeys the laws of science, placed us here on a planet that is uniquely fine-tuned for life as we know it, created order and the scientific constants by which we live, we should be able to study this universe with every faculty and it ought to make sense. It is only natural that theology: the study of God, and science: the study of nature, agree with each other. Science and faith are not polar opposites. We simply live in a world where the rules of science, established by God, continue to function, and only occasionally does God intervene as an outside force to change the natural paths of the universe. Certainly, the initial creation of the universe, call it Big Bang or *de novo* creation, is one of the places where we might expect a creative God to step in. It also seems that God continues to reserve the right to step in as a force from outside the usual bounds of nature such that supernatural events are still happening.

## Chapter 8: Describing Supernatural Experiences

Perhaps you have noticed as I describe supernatural signs and miracles that I have mostly chosen to speak of events that I have either witnessed myself or have had described to me by the person who experienced it. Occasionally I have included a further removed miracle if there was good evidence for the credibility of the story. I have also chosen my words carefully. I do this for two reasons: one is that I am seeking not to create undue influence on the reader to see things in the manner I see them. I want to leave space for the reader to draw their own conclusions about the experiences described. No one can be strong-armed into believing in the existence of miracles or of a creator God. The second reason for carefully choosing my words is that **the very nature of transferring my experience or someone else's experience into words and seeking to describe it to others is an extremely difficult task.**

Teresa of Avila, a Spanish mystic and Carmelite nun who lived from 1515 to 1582, knew that her experiences of God were difficult to explain to others. She claimed to have experienced the supernatural in a number of ways and others saw evidence of supernatural experiences in her life, including divine guidance, deliverance from fear, expressions of peace, ecstatic emotions, trances, and levitation (yes, levitation, as hard as that is for us to believe). We can sense her frustration in trying to explain her experiences in some of her writings. In her book, *The Interior Castle*, she writes:

> I am convinced that those who refuse to believe that God can do far more than this, and that He is pleased now, as in the past, to communicate Himself to His creatures, shut fast their hearts against receiving such favors themselves. Do not imitate them, sisters: be convinced that it is possible for God to perform still greater wonders. Do not concern yourselves as to whether those who receive these graces are good or wicked; as I said, He knows best and it is no business of yours: you should serve Him with a single heart and with humility, and should praise Him for His works and wonders.[45]

Teresa is frustrated yet gracious and recognizes that those who disbelieve her are quite within their rights to disbelieve. It is no business of hers whether or not they believe. Yet she also tells her reader to avoid imitating those who do not believe. She challenges us to consider that God is still pleased to communicate with his people

---

[45] Teresa of Avila, *The Interior Castle*, The Fifth Mansions, Chapter 1, p. 124

even 1500 and more years beyond the experiences of those who lived while Jesus walked the earth. She wants us to know that he is still capable of, and in fact does do, great wonders on the earth.

There are times when I feel the same conflict in my spirit. My desire is to encourage my reader to consider that the triune God is still working wonders, miracles, signs, and the supernatural here on earth in the 21st century. Yet I am well aware of my own limitations in describing things in such a way that will do justice to the great mystery and omniscient power of our God. I am also aware of the limitations of my reader to reach beyond the empirical skepticism of our day and take at face value the things I and others are writing. The time into which we have all been born has led us to look for hidden agendas and ulterior motives behind everything that is written. How will we ever get a fair hearing for the supernatural interventions God chooses to do in our world? What of those who miss the miracles God is doing all around us? **Could we sometimes actually be recipients of miracles and not even recognize them? On the other hand, might we sometimes ascribe to God's power everyday accidents of randomness in a world with many choices and decisions?**

In Chapter Three of this book, I told the story of my strongest candidate for a supernatural miracle: the healing of the mass on the pons of my brain and the disappearance of the coinciding headaches. I have told this story many times to many friends with a variety of responses. I have heard, "sounds like a genuine miracle." I have also heard the nervous laugh and the intended pun, "perhaps it was all in your head." A good friend of mine, a faithful follower of Jesus, who has much faith in a variety of areas, suggested that perhaps my body simply healed itself. To me, God's intervention and my body healing itself might actually be one and the same. Tumors in the brain do not usually heal themselves. But perhaps with a little coaxing from God, our bodies do spontaneously heal.

However, my friend, let's call him Martin, is actually suggesting that the tumor would have resolved, whether or not we had prayed, by the natural mechanisms built into our bodies by the Creator. He may be right; our bodies have remarkable capacities for DNA repair and viral destruction, and even have cells whose purpose is to seek out rogue cancer cells and destroy them. My interpretation that God coaxed the process as he responded to the prayers of God's people may or may not be the correct understanding of what happened. Martin is a pastor who has prayed for God's healing in many circumstances and saw his own son healed of cancer through the difficult process of chemotherapy and significant medical intervention. He and his church prayed consistently for his son and believed that their prayers made a difference in the healing process. However, approximately two years after the cancer was beaten, his son's lungs began to fail due to complications of the chemotherapy and sadly, he died. **How does one retain faith in a loving, supernatural, healing God through such a journey as Martin and his wife have been on? I cannot be critical of my friend's assessment and understanding of the supernatural and the miraculous. I have not been through what he has been through.**

Such is the nature of supernatural occurrences: they are painfully difficult to explain to others. Yet those who have seen unexplainable supernatural events cannot get them out of their minds and wish that they could tell everyone they meet so that they might understand their excitement. What is it in the mind of humans that causes two people to see the same thing and interpret it differently? For now, we must live with these difficulties in explaining our experiences and the miraculous events we have seen. Again, I leave it to the reader to assess whether or not I have constructed a suitable case for others to believe in regular, but uncommon, supernatural events.

Perhaps the ambiguous nature of the supernatural and how difficult it is to explain our experiences to others is part of what points us to God. Kallistos Ware says, "… it is not the task of Christianity to provide easy answers to every question, but to make us progressively aware of a mystery. God is not so much the object of our knowledge as the cause of our wonder."⁴⁶ **What if all of the questions about the natural and supernatural world were designed to point us to the mystery of God?** For God truly is a mystery; not even the greatest theologians of our time would claim to have a complete understanding of the creator. He is beyond our comprehension. Why should we be surprised if his ways of interacting with our world are complex and mysterious?

The psalmist in Psalm 139:6 speaks of God's understanding as being much greater than our own understanding. The writer points out that God knows his heart and what he is going to say before he even says it. Then he says, "Such knowledge is too wonderful for me, too great for me to understand!"

That great example of pain and suffering in the Old Testament of the Bible, Job, knew when to be quiet before God and allow God's wisdom to exceed his own understanding:

> Then Job replied to the Lord:
> "I know that you can do all things;
>   no purpose of yours can be thwarted.
> You asked, 'Who is this that obscures my plans without knowledge?'
>   Surely I spoke of things I did not

---

[46] The Orthodox Way, Bishop Kallistos Ware, SVS Press, 1995.

understand,
> things too wonderful for me to know.
"You said, 'Listen now, and I will speak;
> I will question you,
> and you shall answer me.'
My ears had heard of you
> but now my eyes have seen you.
Therefore I despise myself
> and repent in dust and ashes."[47]

**At the end of the day, I too must trust in the mystery of God. I too must know when to speak and when to hold my tongue, for God's ways continue to be a mystery to his people.**

---

[47] Job 42:1-6 (NIV)

## Chapter 9: Birth of the Pentecostal Movement and the Purpose of Signs

In the first chapter, I mentioned briefly the "Christian-bubble" inside which some have tried to cocoon themselves and stay protected from the age of science in which we otherwise live. They might wish to ignore the controversies of our world and ignore the science of the day. When pressed, they might say that they don't understand science and they simply trust God. They seek to ignore those who say that science explains it all. Before he died in 2018, Steven Hawking proclaimed his belief that we no longer need religion or even philosophy and declared both to be dead disciplines.[48] Philosophers of the day may disagree and say that science has in fact strayed into the realm of philosophy.

Church people through history have had an uneasy relationship with both philosophy and the kind of philosophical science to which Hawking refers. Hawking is of course not simply using science as a tool but expects it to be able to fill in all of the gaps in knowledge including the existence of the universe (or universes), the existence (or non-existence) of God, and other philosophical questions that have plagued humans for millennia.

---

[48]

https://www.theguardian.com/commentisfree/belief/2010/sep/08/stephen-hawking-philosophy-maths

Christians still believe that there are philosophical and theological questions beyond the scope and reach of scientific methodologies. The existence of God is a case in point. **Despite centuries of trying, no one has been able to definitively prove the existence of God. Yet neither has science nor philosophy been able to definitively prove that God does *not* exist. It is the type of question that God has left permanently outside of our knowing.**

So, Christians strive against the kind of science Steven Hawking has come to represent: a triumphalist, certain, atheistic, humanistic science that knows of nothing else and bows to no other conversations. On the other hand, Christians also have struggles with the supernatural. As one traces church history, one of the key elements that caused people to separate into various denominations has been different perspectives on how much we could expect God to work in this world. A question we ask is, "Can we still expect God to heal people of their physical diseases or not?"

Even as we look at the history of the church in the last three to four hundred years, we see that there have been a number of ways in which people have dealt with the ambiguity of the natural and supernatural worlds. The supernaturalism (as a philosophical construct) of the Middle Ages gave way to the philosophical concept of skepticism in the 1600s. Descartes and other philosophers before him had a tremendous impact on society in France and around the world. This way of thinking, in which nothing was trusted nor believed that could not be tested with empirical data, also influenced science and the way in which theologians and church members experienced the miraculous. In an age of skepticism, we see a rise of Cessationism that begins to have a strong hold on the doctrine of a broad spectrum of the church. Consequently, at a certain stage in the history of the church, few were expecting or praying for supernatural solutions to everyday problems. After all, most miracles could be easily explained away using skepticism and science. It became a way to save face with the skeptics of the day. People did not have to look foolish as they appealed to others to believe the miracle they had just witnessed. Many did believe that miracles could theoretically happen, yet they claimed not to have seen any truly supernatural events.

**Yet as the supernatural was marginalized to a greater and greater extent, there was a gentle push-back in some quarters of the Church. Some began to look for miracles in everyday life and began to preach about the signs and wonders of the New Testament, of the Kingdom of God breaking into the kingdom of the earth.** This has happened a few times in the recent history of the church.

Azusa:

At the turn of the 20th century, in Azusa, California, a small group of Christians and their pastor became the pebble dropped into a still pond with ripples that engulfed the world. A humble, soft-spoken African-American pastor named William Joseph Seymour started a movement of charismatic Pentecostal revival. Known mostly for his Bible knowledge and ability to teach, he was a deeply spiritual man who began to teach glossolalia (speaking in languages unknown to the person speaking) as the initial evidence of the Holy Spirit's work in the lives of believers. His message was rejected by much of his church but embraced by a small core of people who met with him in a run-down building in April of 1906. Seymour preached about speaking in tongues and people received the ability to speak in languages unknown to the speaker and to proclaim their faith with greater confidence than they had before. Christians from other parts of the city, state, and country began to attend services and the vigour of the movement swept across the country and around the world creating the world-wide Pentecostal movement. Healing miracles began to be associated with the revival and many believed in the supernatural power of God. Theologians and sociologists alike have studied this movement of revival in the early 1900s and as we read their collective wisdom we are still left with many questions. History does bear out that many hoaxes of healing and religious fervour occurred in this time. Yet there is also evidence that miracles of healing did occur as a result of the quiet and spiritual teaching of Seymour and other early charismatic leaders.

Pentecostalism:

The Azusa movement spread and led to the formation of the Pentecostal movement in the United States and around the world. Denominations such as the Assemblies of God in the U.S. and the Pentecostal Assemblies of God (PAOC) in Canada resulted from the preaching of evangelists who proclaimed the same enduring power of the Holy Spirit as did the early Azusa movement. Today there are approximately 59 million members and adherents of the Worldwide Assemblies of God Fellowship who would attest to the supernatural in-breaking in their history and in their present experience. Many would also bear witness to healing miracles in their lives. Despite the fact that some high-profile healing hoaxes have been seen in this movement, there is a much wider group of more low-key workers and evangelists that saw healings throughout their ministry. Many of the early Pentecostal evangelists had healing as part of their ministry.

Dr. Charles S. Price was a little-known evangelist of the 1920s.[49] Born in Sheffield, England in 1887, Charlie Price spent time in Canada and the U.S.A. He found faith in Jesus through a Free Methodist church in Spokane and took up a career as a minister of the gospel but soon fell into a liberal, Cessationist branch of the church. He was invited to attend an evangelistic meeting in San Jose, California at which Aimee Semple McPherson, an

---

[49] The details of the life of Dr. Charles S. Price are largely taken from *The Story of My Life* by Charles S. Price.

Assemblies of God evangelist, spoke. Price was convinced that McPherson was a fraud and planned to preach a message exposing her fraudulent message the following week in his own pulpit. However, in the course of two days of evangelistic meetings, Price found himself changed by the messages of Aimee Semple McPherson and found himself "saved." Price went from those nights with a greater power from the Holy Spirit, eventually leading evangelistic meetings as a minister of the Congregational Church of California. He was a person of great influence in the early Pentecostal movement in Canada and in British Columbia (B.C.) in particular.

The largest evangelistic services of Charles S. Price were held in Victoria and Vancouver, B.C. in 1923. Price first held services in Victoria, and it is estimated that one-sixth of Victoria's population went to hear him speak at Willows Arena at Oak Bay in April of 1923.[50] Then, for three weeks in May of 1923, Price held evangelistic services in Vancouver at the Denman Arena. Thousands came to hear him, and many attested to miracles of salvation and healing. The meetings in Vancouver had been controversial and some ministers in the city opposed them but the Ministerial Association of Victoria sent a document affirming the value of Dr. Price's influence in their city. Referring to Charles S. Price, the proclamation read in part, "…we would commend, without reserve, the fine Christian spirit, the transparent character, and evident

---

[50] (MDM 2016)

devotion of the evangelist in all his work." The proclamation went on to say that "the prayers offered for the healing of the sick have been answered in many cases that can be verified, and that there are many instances where bodily disease and infirmity have apparently disappeared, and the persons concerned claim to be perfectly well." These and other such evangelistic services of that era lead to the rapid growth of the Pentecostal movement in B.C. and the rest of Canada and attest to the supernatural influence of God in the churches of that day.

Vineyard Movement:
No investigation into the supernatural influence of God would be complete without a brief discussion of John Wimber. Wimber, known as the influential pioneer of The Vineyard Church, preached, wrote books, and taught seminars on the Holy Spirit, physical healings, and *Power Evangelism*. He was considered a wise, yet humble leader in the charismatic movement of the 1980's in North American evangelicalism. He became a Christian at the age of 29 and went on to train at Azusa Pacific College before becoming a pastor at the Yorba Linda Friends Church, Calvary Chapel in Los Angeles, and Vineyard Christian Fellowship in Anaheim. Throughout his life, Wimber preached a gospel of The Kingdom of God and encouraged Christians to expect miracles of healing and signs of God's power.

**Wimber did not attach the healing and miraculous gifts to himself or anyone else in his**

**movement. He was quick to point out the democracy of God. One of his favorite sayings that is still used in the Vineyard Movement of today is, "Everybody gets to play."**[51] What he meant was that God does not play favorites with his followers. Everyone gets their share of opportunities to pray for the miraculous and share in the glory of the healings and the disappointments of disease.

Even as his own health deteriorated, Wimber remained convinced that God was indeed the source of physical healing and that signs and wonders would lead the unbelieving to Jesus. Known for his authenticity, he spoke openly about the struggle of believing in healing as he experienced pain and disease:

> Sometimes our experiences don't fit with our understanding of what the Bible teaches. On the one hand, we know that God is sovereign and that he sent Jesus to commission us to pray for and heal the sick. On the other hand, we know from experience that healing does not always occur. Why would God command us to heal the sick and then choose not to back

---

[51] As I was writing this book, I attended a preaching seminar led by a gifted Vineyard preacher named Joyce Rees and heard one of the assistants in her church quote the line, "Everybody gets to play." I good-naturedly suggested that he might want to credit John Wimber with those words, and he replied, "It's a Vineyard thing."

> up our act (so to speak) by not healing the person for whom we pray? This can be downright discouraging, as I learned years ago in my own congregation when I began to teach on healing. It was nine months before we saw the first person healed. The temptation was to withdraw from practicing Christ's commands or, at the other extreme, to drum up a false bravado to convince God to do what we thought He ought to do.[52]

John Wimber's wife Carol points out that John was practical about people and the church and he suggested that the "outpouring of the Holy Spirit had about a twenty-year life span before people started building monuments to themselves."[53] He went on to say, "I don't expect us to be any different. But the Lord is faithful, and He'll pour out His Spirit again and again. It may not be here, but let's all be watching and listening, and as soon as that happens, let's go where He is!"[54]

Wimber continued to preach flexibility, moving with the Holy Spirit, and doing humble tasks for the poor. His focus on being willing to do menial tasks of service kept him humble even as he saw great miracles in his

---

[52] Wimber, John (1996). *Living with Uncertainty: My Bout with Inoperable Cancer.* Vineyard Ministries.
[53] (DeCenso 2009, 68)
[54] (DeCenso 2009, 68)

ministry. The warmth of this voice, in the midst of many other voices of bravado or discouragement is a welcome tone in the conversations regarding the supernatural.

Christian and Missionary Alliance:
Many denominations have historically gone through periods of heightened supernatural incidence followed by periods in which the supernatural seems to be of lesser importance. A friend of mine in the Christian and Missionary Alliance (C&MA) denomination in Canada points to his own denomination's unsettled perspective on the miraculous and the power of the Holy Spirit. A.B. Simpson, an early leader in the C&MA, taught on the power of the Holy Spirit and healing miracles but eventually came into disagreement with some of the teachings of the early Pentecostal movement. In later years, the C&MA denomination wrote papers encouraging leaders to "seek not, forbid not"[55] when it came to the gift of tongues and some of the other more dramatic expressions of the Holy Spirit in the church. Ever since that time the denomination has wrestled with the interpretation of these words and has tried to find a middle road on the question of the supernatural. Some leaders have been known to be Cessationists while others emphasise teaching on the miraculous and both extremes seem to move in waves through this large Canadian denomination, taking turns at being the leading idea.

---

[55] "Where We Stand," Alliance Witness 98 (May 1, 1963), 19.

I doubt that this perspective within the C&MA is unique to this denomination. I would suggest that most denominations and networks of churches ride this same roller coaster. **It is as if the human spirit needs to see signs, wonders, and miracles to keep us in the faith, and so God visits us from time to time with a fresh batch of miracles** from his supernatural treasure chest. Or perhaps God functions the same as he did many years ago, but we perceive him differently, based on where we are at in our spiritual journey. It is helpful to note that currently, there is an increased interest in the supernatural in the Catholic Church. In April of 2018, Pope Francis gave a weekly address in which he spoke of the spiritual battle in which the faithful engage against the devil.[56] The Catholic Church has always maintained a significant emphasis on the healing miracles, signs, wonders, and exorcisms.[57]

I am not a denominational leader and I will tread carefully here lest it seem that I am criticizing any particular denomination or network of churches (including my own), but I wonder if individual churches and denominations need to ask some difficult questions about the link between signs, wonders, and the

---

56

https://www.catholic.org/news/hf/faith/story.php?id=77247
April 26, 2018 weekly address of the Pope.

[57] https://www.catholicnewsagency.com/news/us-exorcists-demonic-activity-is-on-the-rise-45102

supernatural, and the growth rate of our churches and denominations. **Could it be that the lack of growth in some of our churches and denominations is actually a product of the way in which we have ignored the supernatural?** What if we asked for, looked for, and expected to see the supernatural in our churches? Might we see more life? Might we see more growth?

In the New Testament, Jesus' miracles are often referred to as signs and wonders and they did much to attract people and point them to the Kingdom of God. **Signs point to something more.** In the case of Jesus, his signs and wonders pointed ahead to the ultimate wonder, his resurrection from the dead. Today miracles are signs of the future return of Jesus and signs of our hope of eternal life. We must consider how important it may be to see the signs that point toward the eternal hope of the resurrection. Is this something worth the consideration of all Christians as we seek to tell the full truth of the Gospel?

## Chapter 10: Walking in the Dark

Much of this book has been a logical examination of what we might see in this world that points toward the reality of a supernatural, unseen world. The supernatural world, if it exists at all, is indeed unseen. The creator of the universe may step into the visible world and create changes in the physical world from time to time, but for the most part, he is totally invisible and undetectable. I have stayed focused on the logical arguments that we use in everyday conversation as we consider whether or not something exists and have asked us to consider opening our minds to the possibility that God might exist and that he does indeed intervene in the world in supernatural ways.

In this chapter, I want to appeal to both our minds and our hearts. There is more to this question than pure logic and skepticism. Many of us can go through life without seeing miraculous events. Bart Campolo and my friend Robert have lost the ability to see anything that might look like the supernatural. **This might be because they have trained themselves to *not* see the supernatural. Or perhaps, like many of us, they have not trained their minds to look *for* the miraculous.** We live in a world that has coached us to look at certain things and ignore others. Our majority culture has written a script and we play our part in the drama. There is no room in this script for certain experiences, interpretations, or perspectives on reality. When we ask bigger questions and wonder about where the universe came from and if there might not indeed be a creator behind it, we have gone off script and our majority culture has no room for these questions and views of the world. If we choose to embrace a supernatural reality, we must transform our minds such that they are receptive to the messages of the supernatural world. Previously, I quoted C.S. Lewis who spoke of humans as being amphibians who are born into a physical world in which we prepare ourselves for living in a spiritual world. To live in that spiritual world, we must train our spiritual lungs to live in the spiritual world. We must train our minds to see the supernatural world. Walter Brueggemann is saying something similar in one of his writings:

> We now know that human transformation does not happen through didacticism or through excessive certitude, but through the playful entertainment of another scripting of reality that may subvert the old given text and its interpretation and lead to the embrace of an alternative text and its redescription of reality.[58]

---

[58] Walter Brueggemann, *Cadences of Home*

I want to take the reader on a journey in which we consider this redescription of reality. I encourage us to **use our sense of wonder to reclaim an alternative text that allows for the interaction of God.** It is the kind of journey I have been taking all of my life.

Darkness is not as easy to come by as it once was. At least not the literal kind. When I grew up on a small farm in central Alberta the nights were truly dark. Most people turned off all lights on their farm when they went to bed. There were very few mercury-vapour yard lights in the area (the kind that can light up a whole yard like a street light in the city). The cities were smaller and did not give off as much light pollution. The night skies were spectacular. I remember standing in the yard and being awestruck by the immensity of the Milky Way. In one swath across the sky I could see thousands of distant stars all at once. I imagined what it would be like to travel to a distant star or to some exotic planet. I learned the names of a few constellations and stars and loved to watch for them in the sky: Ursa Major, Ursa Minor, Orion, Cassiopeia, Polaris. Each had a wonderful name that rolled off the tongue and allowed me to dream of places far, far away. I soon learned that the Big Dipper (Ursa Major) and the Little Dipper (Ursa Minor) could help me find direction. As long as I could see these stars, and the North Star (Polaris) to which they pointed, I could always know north and, by inference, south, east, and west. With this knowledge I would surely be able to find my way home.

Darkness and light (Matthew 4:16; John 1:5; and Psalm 119:105), seeing dimly as through a mirror (1 Corinthians 13:12), beginning to see again (Mark 8:24, 25), and seeing by faith (2 Corinthians 5:7): these are the metaphors of the seen and unseen spiritual world. The Apostle John calls us to "walk in the light" (1 John 1:5-7) and so it is not surprising that we are drawn to light and fearful of darkness. In a spiritual sense, we feel a greater need to call upon God for his supernatural help when we walk in darkness. As my thoughts return to my childhood, the context of God's word regarding light and darkness helps me understand how God used small pinpoints of light to draw me toward him.

Orion was always a favourite constellation of mine. As a child, noticing this collection of stars but not knowing it by name, I had given it my own moniker: "The Scotty Dog." Years later in high school a science teacher brought in his photos of his favourite constellations and I discovered that my little "Scotch Terrier in the sky" was actually Orion The Hunter, with bow, arrow, and a belt of three stars. I often stared out the window of the car, gazing at Orion, as our family drove home from town. I would try to imagine how long it had taken the light of those stars to reach my eyes. By the time I was 15 I knew that light from even the closest stars had to travel many years to reach earth. Light that I was seeing shining from the centre star of Orion's belt had left that star over 1300 years before I sat in my parents' car watching it twinkle in the night sky. When the photons of light that were now exciting the nerve cells in my retina had left that star the ancient Anglo-Saxon poet, Caedmon, was composing hymns of praise to the creator of these stars in a cattle shed attached to an abbey on the coast of the North Sea in what is now known as Scotland. Ever since that time, around 675 CE, those photons of light had been travelling through the vast distances of space to reach my eye. **It was almost impossible to understand this, and it filled me with awe and pointed me to God.** As I gazed out the window my mind was filled with questions. Why was there so much space out there? What were those distant stars and planets like? Was there life on any of those planets? Could there be intelligent life that was looking back at me and wondering if there was life "out there"? These were some of my first thoughts about exobiology, thoughts I would come back to many more times in the future.

Those were the days of the Apollo space program and every kid dreamed of being an astronaut. In 1969 when Apollo 11 landed in the Sea of Tranquility I remember looking for that place on the face of the moon and wondering, if I squinted really hard, might I see the men walking around in their space suits or see bits and pieces of space junk they had left behind? My imagination soared as I rode my bike on dirt paths and dreamed that I was riding a spaceship through the solar system and landing on interesting planets.

The displays of Aurora borealis, or the northern lights, were also particularly spectacular in the winters of my youth. I would stand for long periods of time watching the greenish blue curtains of light in the sky and imagine that I could hear them snapping and sizzling in the night. Scientists now tell me that the sounds I thought I heard, on those silent nights as I watched the swish of lights, were literally all in my head. Scientists tell me that when we are really quiet, we can sense electrical impulses in our brains as our eyes respond to the intense colours of the aurora in front of us. This electrical leakage from the brain is detected by our auditory systems and we "hear" the chemo-electric impulses that match the motion of the lights as they move and affect our visual systems.

Today most of us see stars very infrequently and many have never seen the northern lights. Even at a distance of many miles from the nearest city, the light pollution from urban centres destroys our ability to see all but the brightest stars which, in turn, makes constellations very difficult to discern. For hundreds and thousands of years humans have looked up at these stars and wondered what they meant. Ours is one of the first generations to actually know the composition of a star and where it is in the universe. We are also one of the first generations to live most of the time not seeing the stars. An application on my phone allows me to point my phone at the stars and identify the ones I see within a computer-generated overlay of all of the stars I might possibly see. It is very disheartening to notice all of the stars that could be seen hundreds of years ago when the constellation maps were created and compare it to the pittance of stars available to me on a clear night in Western Canada. **Many people go through their lives without contemplating the immensity of space because we so rarely see the stars. Could this be one of the reasons why faith in a creator God is waning?** Whole generations of children have grown up in cities in which they can only see one or two stars at a time. They may never know the awe of the Milky Way or the beauty of the Aurora borealis or think about the vast distances of space. How different would I be today without having my imagination stimulated by the beauty of a prairie sky at night? Nights like that are never forgotten. Even today when I look up at Orion it still looks like "The Scotty Dog" to me.

For a number of years, I have developed a spiritual practise of going for walks in the dark. That is, I like to go for walks at night in places that are as dark as possible. When I lived in a large urban centre like Vancouver there were plenty of city lights. So, in my quest for darkness I found myself walking in places like beaches, parks, and the Iona Jetty. The Iona Jetty is a 4.5 km pier built to contain a treated water outflow. It is a popular place for cyclists and walkers. It allows one to walk or cycle approximately 4 km out into the Strait of Georgia. Walking there at night you can get away from the lights of the city and the shoreline. It is one of the best places in Greater Vancouver to see the stars. It is also dark enough to be a bit eerie. One comes upon the occasional Great

Blue Heron sleeping with its head tucked down toward its breast and other shore birds splash and squawk along the pier. Then there are the planes. Because the jetty is very close to the Vancouver International Airport and directly along the flight path of certain runways, a night walker will sometimes be startled by the landing lights and roar of a large plane flying low directly overhead.

I have also lived in Calgary and one of my favourite places to go for a night walk is a retreat centre near Calgary called King's Fold. It is a fantastic retreat centre for individual retreats or small groups. It is set on the banks of the Ghost River and guests can stay in the main lodge or one of the hermitages built in secluded spots. At night one can hike the river valley with just the light of the stars as a guide. The valley of the Ghost River is a wonderful habitat for deer as well as large predators such as bears and cougars. One must be cautious and listen for approaching animals.

The first time I intentionally set out to walk in the dark at King's Fold was during a solo retreat in which I was seeking to hear from God about my future. My wife, a few friends, and I had started a new church in Calgary, and it was well-established and ready for others to lead. My wife Maureen and I had just made the decision to move from Calgary to Vancouver to start another church. It felt risky and dangerous. It meant selling our large home in Calgary where we had raised our three daughters. It meant buying a small condo in downtown Vancouver. It meant running the risk that we might fail. It meant Maureen would need to leave a great job, with no sure jobs in Vancouver. There were many uncertainties and few sure things in the series of events into which we walked.

So, I went for a night walk. There were lanterns and flashlights available, but I opted to walk without lights. I remember praying and asking God to help me to trust him in dangerous, risky situations. I prayed about what it must have been like for the biblical shepherd David who watched over sheep at night while predators tried to steal from the herd or attack him in the dark. I trusted God to protect me from cougars while I walked through the dense trees of this river valley. I told God that I wanted to live a life of risk for the sake of the work to which he would call me. I told him I was willing to take risks and that I would trust him to take care of me and my family and that whatever came my way I would receive it from his hand as a gift. I thought of David who as a young boy fought against a mighty warrior named Goliath. I thought of the way David trusted God in dangerous situations. In 1 Samuel 17:32-37 we read:

> "Don't worry about this Philistine," David told Saul. "I'll go fight him!" "Don't be ridiculous!" Saul replied. "There's no way you can fight this Philistine and possibly win! You're only a boy, and he's been a man of war since his youth."

But David persisted. "I have been taking care of my father's sheep and goats," he said.
"When a lion or a bear comes to steal a lamb from the flock, I go after it with a club and rescue the lamb from its mouth. If the animal turns on me, I catch it by the jaw and club it to death. I have done this to both lions and bears, and I'll do it to this pagan Philistine, too, for he has defied the armies of the living God! The Lord who rescued me from the claws of the lion and the bear will rescue me from this Philistine!"

As I walked in the Ghost River Valley, there *was* an element of fear. The hair on the back of my neck stood on end and I felt myself tensing with every tiny noise of a mouse in the grass or an owl in the distance. Night walks heighten my senses and allow me to listen better, smell more, and detect things I might normally miss. One must overcome a sense of fear. From birth, most of us are taught to be afraid of the dark. There was also a sense of peace. I was trusting God to keep me safe and rescue me from real dangers. God was very much present on these walks and he spoke to me in the quiet of that night. He spoke peace and reassurance into my mind. He called on me to trust him and to be willing to risk all for the sake of speaking peace, hope, and joy into the lives of others. My sleep that night was deep and peaceful, and I awoke refreshed and ready to take on all that the world might throw at me.

At breakfast I spoke with one of the staff members at the retreat centre. She told me of an experience she had had the previous week. In daylight hours, she came around a corner on the riverbank path and was face to face with a cougar. This was an unusual event since cougars are largely nocturnal and it is rare to see one out in the mid-day sun. She was walking with the retreat dog, which immediately began to growl and bark at the big cat. The mountain lion had, in turn, growled and hissed back. As dog and cat stared each other down, the staff member had slowly backed away and headed back up the path away from the site of the encounter. The old dog soon followed. The dangers of these riverbank paths were very real. Someone later found a dead deer that had been brought down by the cougar. It was more than the big cat could eat all at once and so it was likely hanging around guarding its precious food supply.

Walking in the dark is the metaphor that I want to keep before me for the rest of my life. The life I live in Canada is really quite safe and secure. Most of the time I organize my life in ways that protect me and minimize my exposure to danger or the risk of loss. I have my keys and locks to keep out the "bad-guy," "bogeyman," and "terrorist." I have my vitamins and disinfectants to protect me from disease and bed bugs. I have my real estate, life insurance, Registered Savings Plans, and stock investments to placate my fear of the financial future. I am fortunate to have so much. Many in the world have none of these things. They survive and thrive without all of these protections. Could I do as well if I were to lose all of my security blankets? **Walking in the dark with an element of danger is a way to remind myself that I cannot trust in my securities.** It humbles me and brings me to a place where I begin to look at where my hope rests. It reminds me that life is about risk; it is about taking chances when every fibre of my body cries out for comfort and security. I am brought once again to the realization that it is a remarkable stroke of grace that our universe exists, that our earth is capable of life, and that I can walk freely about on this earth. Without this common grace from a creator God I would not even be in this place where I could choose an element of risk and danger. It reminds me to put my trust in the right places.

Walking in the dark allows me to see things that stimulate my imagination and keep me looking toward God. Stars and seashores and moonbeams are the beginnings of songs and poetry and works of art. The smell of a wood smoke fire on a dark and cool night triggers primordial shared human memories and sparks thoughts of home, food, and well-earned comfort. Walking in the dark reminds me that I am small and fragile in a big world of danger. **It causes me to dream big and have greater vision for the way things could be. It causes me to pray and trust and love and hunger for**

**something more.** It reminds me that life is about risk; it is about taking chances when every fibre of my body cries for comfort and security. Where would I be if I had never taken a chance? Where would I be today if I had taken more chances in life?

Walking in the dark reminds me that there are more sources of light than sunshine, streetlights, and flashlights. There is inner light and that light is a reflection of light that is far greater. There is a light in which we can walk that will bring light to any dark place. Isaiah 60:19 says, "No longer will you need the sun to shine by day, nor the moon to give its light by night, for the Lord your God will be your everlasting light, and your God will be your glory." 1 John 1:5-7 says:

> This is the message we heard from Jesus and now declare to you: God is light, and there is no darkness in him at all. So we are lying if we say we have fellowship with God but go on living in spiritual darkness; we are not practicing the truth. But if we are living in the light, as God is in the light, then we have fellowship with each other, and the blood of Jesus, his Son, cleanses us from all sin.

As we walk in physical darkness; as we walk through circumstances of life that are risky, dangerous, and dark; as we walk forward without clearly seeing where we are going; we can be guided by the One who is light and in whom there is no darkness. He is our guide. He does not promise that we will always be kept safe in every dangerous or risky situation. Otherwise, could we explain the many horrible things that happen to people as they are in the midst of trusting the God of light and creation? He does not ask us to risk our lives every moment of the day. He is not calling us to be foolhardy. Perhaps this metaphor is more about recognizing that we are constantly in danger. If it were not for God's continuous sustaining presence in the life of every person on this planet, none of us could survive. The metaphor is about living inside of this reality. What does it mean to walk in the dark in good times, in difficult times, in times of success and in times of failure, in times of great joy and in times of pain and suffering?

I continue to let this metaphor resonate and see how it applies in various situations in life and in the life of others who have chosen to risk rather than stay in the safe zone. It is a message that is needed in the places I have lived. So much of what I have heard from the television, news services, and my peers has given me a very different message. The dominant voice in our culture is about protection, safety, and avoiding risk. We are told to protect ourselves and our homes, avoid those things or people who might do us harm, and get a good return on our investments. What I am suggesting here is that we need to explore risk, explore faith, trust God in difficult times, find creativity in life, find God in everyday places, listen to the right voices, and take risks for the sake of others, while looking for God's guidance in the midst of risk.

At a very practical level, what I am suggesting is a strategy of life that leaves opportunity for the supernatural to break into the natural. If we never look for gold, how would we know whether or not it was there in the mud at our feet? If we never look for hints of the supernatural, how will we ever see it in the physical reality of this world? If we want to see supernatural events, we will need to retrain our minds to recognize that although we live in a physical world that demands our attention, there is an unseen spiritual world that is just as real as the physical world: "…we fix our gaze on things that cannot be seen. For the things we see now will soon be gone, but the things we cannot see will last forever" (2 Corinthians 4:18). Our eyes, our spirits, our hearts, dare I say, our imaginations, need to be trained to watch for the influence of this world that cannot be seen. When we walk in the dark, our other four senses become heightened and we rely heavily upon them to guide our steps. **So too it is only by exercising our faith that we learn to walk in the reality of the unseen spiritual world, straining with all of our senses to experience the supernatural.**

## Chapter 11: When miracles don't happen

Clearly, there are times when God is silent. Sometimes we ask for miracles and we receive a clear *no* or hear nothing at all. Let us turn to some of those stories and see if we can work out a sense of what is happening at times like this.

From 2003 through 2008, I was the organizer and pastor of a network of house churches in Calgary. Within this collection of followers of Jesus, we saw many answers to prayer and examples of the supernatural. During the nearly two years that the Siparia family was part of one of those house church gatherings, they had experienced a number of challenges. They had been loved and supported through the death of the grandfather of the family and then they struggled with the poor health of their grandma. The network of house churches and their particular gathering became a surrogate family for these immigrants from Trinidad.

One incident in the life of the Siparia family serves as an example of what we may experience as we pray, look for supernatural intervention, and hear only silence from God. In 2005, the grandmother, Renata, developed a serious infection in her foot that reduced circulation and threatened her life. The doctors suggested that the foot would need to be amputated and the church community began to pray that God might save the foot. Many people prayed, many people believed and hoped for a miraculous intervention, and for a while it looked like God had answered that prayer. The doctors felt that with a little more antibiotic treatment and hydrotherapy they could prevent an amputation. The church rejoiced and praised God for his miraculous intervention. We began to tell the story of a supernatural intervention and our faith was strengthened. However, a few days later the doctors determined that the therapy was not making enough of a difference and that the amputation would need to be performed to save Renata's life. We were all deflated.

This challenged the faith of all in the group, but our daughter, a 15-year-old at the time, expressed it best when she said, "It feels like God is teasing us! It looked like God was going to answer our prayer for healing and then He didn't." These words of my daughter replayed in my mind for several days and I ruminated on them wondering what I should do to encourage her fragile faith. I looked for explanations and peace and found very little. My daughter and I decided we should go and visit Renata in the hospital and share our disappointment and how this experience was shaking our faith in a God of miracles. As we visited with her we poured out our hearts to her just as we had poured out our hearts to God. We were honest, angry, frustrated, and questioning. **Renata, a woman of great faith, taught my daughter, me, and indeed our entire community a great deal that day when she said, "If we look at the Bible, we see that many people had**

**trials and tribulations. Why would we not expect the same? I have already said goodbye to this foot. I will have a new one in heaven."** We were astounded by Renata's words. They were just what we needed at that time and, although these words did not answer all of our questions about why there is suffering and pain in the world, we could not help but marvel at the words of this woman who could so easily say goodbye to her foot.

The Sunday evening after Renata returned home from the hospital, following the amputation, she and her family still wanted us to have church in their home. Her bed was in one corner of the living room to allow her to function on the main level of the house. As she sat up and told us her story of faith and what God had been teaching her through these experiences, she was surrounded by 30 attentive people who wanted to hear a message from God. Children, teens, young adults, and older adults listened intently. The Holy Spirit spoke through the Bible and through the life of this committed believer that evening. She gave us hope for a good future in the midst of the temporary struggles of this life. She gave us hope of new feet in heaven.

The story goes on a little further. Because Renata was in the process of immigrating to Canada, she did not yet have medical coverage for the hospital bills that added up to more than $40,000. Renata's house church family (and some from the broader house church network) gave more than $13,000 to a trust fund to help with these medical expenses. After the initial payments were made, the group continued to walk with the family as they worked through the immigration process and made payments on the remaining bills.

Was God at work in the life of this family? Did God intervene? Certainly, God did not provide the supernatural miracle of healing that we expected in this situation. Did a community of faith grow in their appreciation of pain, suffering, sickness, community care, and the nature of God? Most certainly. This was an example of "believing when we could not see" (John 20:24-29). It is not as convincing or rewarding as some of the other supernatural stories I have told in this book, but perhaps it has a better message for us than if God had rescued one grandmother's foot.

Indeed, we must ask the difficult questions of faith and the supernatural. I am well aware that my friend Robert, the secular humanist, might point to this situation and say that we Christians are delusional. He would say that we see the miraculous when it is not there and that when we can't see a supernatural healing, we create excuses for God and see other "miracles" in the story. We Christians indeed are open to this criticism and we are sometimes guilty of such manipulation of the interpretation of circumstances. I do not want to sugarcoat our understandings and exaggerate how God works in our world. **The reality is, much of the time, we do not understand the answers to our prayers. We**

**do not understand why we get a *yes* sometimes and a *no* at other times. In fact, sometimes all we get is silence.**

When God is silent, some will believe that those praying and/or those being prayed for must not have had enough faith for the miracle. But this begs the question, "How much faith is enough?" How would one ever know how much faith one person had and how much another didn't have? And of course, we must ask the next question, "Isn't that sort of thinking guilt-inducing?" If I did not have enough faith to get my prayer answered, how poor is my faith? Would God really want me to feel that way? No, there has to be more to this.

Some will want to divide the world into those who deserve a miracle and those who do not deserve a miracle. They will think that those who follow Jesus will get miracles and those who don't follow Jesus do not deserve a miracle. Yet we see no such distinction in the Bible. Jesus heals and helps and teaches every type of person he meets. We see him heal royal officials, people possessed by unclean spirits, a leper who had never met Jesus, the centurion's servant (neither the centurion nor his servant seem to be deserving or seem to be following Jesus), a widow's son, and a synagogue ruler's daughter. We also know that there would have been many who could have used a miracle that did not get one from Jesus. Why did he not heal everyone at the Pool of Bethesda (John 5:1-15)? **It can't be about who deserves a miracle**

**or who is following Jesus or who is not following Jesus.**

Earlier in this book I spoke of my friend Jason who, faced with multiple myeloma, did not receive a healing miracle in this life, while it seemed that I did receive a healing miracle. How do we make sense of this? Many could point to situations in which faithful, praying people have asked for miracles and, by our logic, should have received a miracle. The system does not seem fair, logical or understandable. The logic of such circumstances is what has driven people like Bart Campolo away from God. In a completely consistent and logical system, every prayer would be answered based on the exact same logical and transparent criteria. When we prayed for a miracle, we would know the answer as we prayed it. We would know which circumstances would result in an answer of *yes*, and which circumstances would result in a *no*. Perhaps God does have such a consistent and logical system in the spiritual world and perhaps he is guiding his decisions based upon a particular system that, if we knew of it, we would understand and praise his intelligence for developing such a system. But as it stands now, we cannot see such a system. We ask for the supernatural and it is a mystery as to how God will answer our pleas. Does this mean we should give up on prayer altogether? Does this mean that there is no supernatural, no miraculous? No, it simply means that, for now, we only know partial answers. We cannot see the whole picture (1 Corinthians 13:9).

It also means that we must guard our hearts against bitterness when we see one receiving a healing and another not being healed. The parable Jesus told in Matthew 20:1-16 is instructive here. It is the parable of the vineyard workers. Some are hired early in the morning, some late morning, some mid-day, and two other groups later into the afternoon. At the end of the day when it is time to pay the workers, every one of them receives a full day's pay. Of course, a full day's pay was perfectly fair for those who had worked a full day and they would not have expected more. Perhaps this is how it is for those who never see a miracle in their lives. They receive their reward in heaven: eternal life and all it entails as a free gift of Jesus. A full day's pay was not usually given when a person did not work a full day, but in the case of these vineyard workers they were given full pay regardless of how much of the day they had worked. The vineyard owner was free to give them more than they earned. We might also say this of all who receive eternal life in the Kingdom of God because all are given more than they deserve. Verse 15 asks the interesting question, "Should you be jealous because I am kind to others?" The obvious answer to both the vineyard owner and to our God is "no," we should not be jealous because he is kind to others. Those who do not see a specific miracle in their life can still have a full reward: eternal life with the Lord of the universe. We need not be bitter about situations we do not understand accurately, nor about the generosity of our God. Our Lord is still mysterious and hard to understand this side of heaven. We do not want to be jealous of what he does for or gives to others, just as we would not want others to be jealous of what he has done for us and given to us. God is sovereign in how he chooses to intervene with the supernatural. We cannot fully understand the mind of God.

The stories of miracles written in this book and those handed down through history are always incomplete. The crippled man healed by Jesus at the Pool of Bethesda (John 5:1-15) was healed but we do not know what his life was like after that. After a lifetime of begging and waiting to be healed, how would he make a living in the world? Was there a construction project on which he could use his newfound legs and dig trenches or lay stones? What happened to the 12-year-old girl Jesus raised from the dead (Luke 8:40-56)? We are told that her parents were overwhelmed, but what of the girl? Did she understand what had happened to her? How did she live her life from that point forward? One day she would die again; would someone be there to raise her back to life? Did she grow to be a great saint of the church or did she begin to think that she must have simply fallen into a rather deep sleep? Did she die an old woman or did some other disease take her life a few years later?

In Chapter Five I recounted the story of Tim Stafford's friend, Jeff, who received healing in his feet. How did he deal with the healing he had received? Did it change his life? What are the implications of the restoration of hearing in my friend James Smithman's life?[59] **These are the questions that result from healings and there are many more questions that result from silence. Either way, God is mysterious.**

Knowing that we don't know is small comfort. It is particularly small comfort when a loved one dies or when we or someone we care about suffers from a difficult disease, is abused, bullied, or harassed. I told a story of our daughter who received a miracle of an averted miscarriage. What of all of the women who suffer physically and emotionally painful miscarriages? It can't be because of lack of faith. It can't be that one daughter of God deserves a miracle and another daughter of God does not deserve a miracle. The pain in writing these words leads me to tears for those who have lost a child or lost a loved one because they did not get a miracle. How do we deal with the pain of such circumstances? **There are no simple answers when God is silent and the supernatural breakthrough we had prayed for, hoped for, and believed in does not come.** How does one find peace in such difficult times?

Perhaps one of the best ways to deal with the silence of God is to recognize it as temporary. Historically speaking, we know that in the life of the people of Israel, there was a period of 400 years in which God was largely silent. Between the time of the last authors of the Old Testament and the first authors of the New Testament lies

---

[59] See chapter five.

a 400-year stretch of very few miracles, very few words from God, and very little rescue. God, for the most part, did not speak to his beloved children. Yet even this long stretch of silence was temporary. Just as the last prophets had proclaimed, Jesus bursts onto the scene in a tiny stable in Bethlehem and a period of deafening answers to prayer is inaugurated by his life.

That is how most of us experience God. There will be stretches of silence. Even as I have spoken of miracles in my life, I am well-aware of many years with no miraculous intervention. Times such as these may be short, or they may be long, but there will be stretches of silence between the times when we hear from God. I have suggested that in my life, I may have experienced five to ten supernatural miracles. You may say that is a lot or you may say that is only a few. Either way, we must recognize long periods of silence in my 58 years of life. Through all that time I prayed with similar faith as when the miracles came. But God was silent. We need to see that God's voice is not a cacophony like that of noisy crows roosting in trees. Perhaps his answers are carefully chosen to fit just the right times and places in our spiritual journey. Perhaps they are given when we are most ready to hear and most ready to act upon what we hear and the answers we are given. Silence is temporary.

If you feel that you have never heard from God, if you feel that he has always been silent to you, this too may be temporary. It may be that there has not yet been a time when God felt it appropriate to give you a more obvious and clear answer to your prayers or more clear guidance in your life. Do not be afraid to wait in this temporary silence. However, for most of us, it is not that God has been silent all of our lives, it is more likely that we simply want to hear more from him. Again, we must wait in this temporary silence for the answers that will come at a later time. It may be tomorrow, it may be next month, or it may be years from now that we hear a clear answer from God. The clear answer may only come when we have received a complete healing in heaven. Yet the silence is temporary.

## Chapter 12: Why do we long for something more?

C.S. Lewis is well-known for logical and persuasive arguments that have helped many to believe in God. One of his more famous quotes has to do with why we long for more. He put it this way in *Mere Christianity*:

> Creatures are not born with desires unless satisfaction for those desires exist. A baby feels hunger: well, there is such a thing as food. A duckling desires to swim: well, there is such a thing as water. Men feel sexual desire: well, there is such a thing as sex. If I find in myself a desire, which no experience in this world can satisfy, the most probable explanation is that I was made for another world. If none of my earthly pleasures satisfy it that does not prove that the universe is a fraud. Probably earthly pleasures were never meant to satisfy it, but to arouse it, to suggest the real thing.[60]

Lewis' argument is a good one (although his comment about sexual desire betrays the patriarchal culture in which he lived), but it is more of a metaphor

---

[60] (Lewis, Mere Christianity 2015, 137)

than a true representation of life. Not everyone will be satisfied by this argument. The obvious issue with it is that it certainly is possible to have desires that are not meant to be fulfilled. If I desire to breathe underwater, it does not mean that I will be able to breathe like a fish. Still, Lewis is expressing **the feeling that many of us sense: that the beautiful desires and emotions we feel point to something more.** In this regard, perhaps we are not all the same. In Chapter Ten, I spent some time suggesting that we may need to develop our imagination to experience all that there is in this world and to sense the feeling of something more. Some of us are more naturally inclined to experience life from a spiritual perspective, but I am convinced that this spiritual perspective can be developed in any one of us.

A few years ago, I had one of those experiences that I find hard to explain that points to something more. I found myself deeply moved by a song. I had just finished a day of work and I was waiting for my wife Maureen, as she was walking home from work. I was sitting in our condo on the 14th floor of a 27-storey skyscraper watching the sun go down and the people bustling home from work. I turned on a previously recorded television show of Jim Cuddy performing his "Set List in Studio One" at Corus Quay in Toronto. He was singing "Skyscraper Soul"[61] and the words flowed over my

---

[61] Rather than quote the song in full, I encourage the reader to read the lyrics and listen to the song online. You can find

consciousness. It was like he was in the room with me describing the sights and feelings as I looked out the window to the streets of Vancouver far below. The words of the song speak of the difficulty of living in the city and how the singer knows the struggles of his neighbours as he sees them looking through the "market stalls." Yet, Cuddy says, he could never leave the city because he has a skyscraper soul. He is attracted to this life in the city. I recall how deeply his words moved me as I looked out at the people below my building scrambling around like ants with too much to do and fears of being stepped on by entities larger than themselves.

I wondered why I was so moved. It was like Jim Cuddy had tapped into my consciousness and wrote my feelings into his poetry. The experience pointed me to universal feelings hidden in the human soul. I realized that Cuddy and I, despite our philosophical differences, were very much the same. It seemed to me in that moment that what we had each experienced was a longing placed in our souls by a God who was bigger than both of us. Our consciousness, emotions, fears, wonders, and joy all seemed to point, in that very moment, to something beyond me, something beyond Jim Cuddy, and something beyond every singer-songwriter and every person on the planet. Not everyone will be able to relate to what I am trying to describe, and, as I said in chapter eight, it is very

---

Cuddy's music here:
https://www.jimcuddy.com/discography/skyscraper-soul/

difficult to describe our emotions and feelings of wonder when we witness a miracle or something unusual from God, but **I do think we can all relate to the idea that there are moments when we are moved so deeply that we feel there has to be something more.**

Music is often a catalyst for me. Sometimes I might be moved by a particularly good guitar solo, the string quartet backing up the other musicians, or a soaring gospel choir filling in a few chords. Some will find my choice of music odd and will say that classical music, or opera, or jazz, or Christian worship music are the types of music that move them beyond the everyday of life. Science has shown that the brain has particular locations that are moved by music. The science as of yet is incomplete and not nearly as specific as researchers would like, but there are certainly some areas of the auditory cortex and the *planum temporale* that are stimulated to a significant degree when one appreciates a piece of music and is moved by it. I have experienced a particular twinge in a consistent region of my brain as I really listen and allow myself to be taken over by the emotions of a particular piece of music. Researchers have found that people with Alzheimer's Disease can often sing the lyrics of songs they learned even though they can't remember more significant things about their life. Stroke patients who cannot form proper sentences in everyday speech can sing a favourite lyric. I have often joked with my children that even if I get Alzheimer's Disease and they ship me off to a nursing home, I will be the happy old man in the corner singing all of the lyrics to Barry Manilow's *Copacabana*.

But it is not only music that can stir us to an emotional experience of powers greater than the physical world. Something as simple as looking at a sunrise over the mountains might be the driving force that points us to the God of the universe. Perhaps it is the love we feel for a newborn son or daughter when we hold them for the first time. Whatever it might be for you, there is likely something that we have all experienced that points us to something more.

Many people, when asked if they have ever seen anything unnatural, odd, or supernatural, have some sort of story to tell. They might wonder about how they managed to survive a car wreck and might say something like, "I guess someone was watching out for me that day." They might refer to a prayer offered and a miraculous answer. They may simply say that they have seen odd things in the world that do not seem to fit with a natural explanation of the world. Most of us have a sense of something more, and even the most ardent agnostic will admit to hoping that a deceased loved one is in a better place. Is this the hand of God reaching out to us and inviting us to look for something more? Are such experiences purely natural or is there an element of the supernatural involved? We must all look to our own experiences and answer questions such as these.

Perhaps the issue is partly about how we tune our minds. Are some minds more naturally tuned to watch for the supernatural and the spiritual? Can we train our minds to watch for the "something more" of this world? Certainly, it takes commitment to keep our minds vigilant and expectant of the supernatural. Perhaps such vigilance is worthwhile. Perhaps this is exactly what it takes to get through this life.

In 2009, I went to the movie theatre to see a Coen brothers' movie on a Saturday night. It was called *A Serious Man* and was a dark comedy about how we understand our existence and the meaning of life. As the directors are Jewish, they have drawn heavily from their understanding of Jewish faith, customs, and the nominal Jewish culture of the 1960s. The movie contained a message like many other Hollywood movies, which might best be summed up in the words of a Grace Slick, Jefferson Airplane song played incessantly throughout the movie: "When the truth is found to be lies and all the joy within you dies, don't you want somebody to love?"[62] The main character gets hit by Job-like catastrophes, has a King David moment on the roof of his house, and finds himself questioning all he has ever believed. The Coens insist upon an absence of meaning in the universe and that the only answers lie in having a good hedonistic time with sex, drugs, and rock 'n roll.

---

[62] "Somebody to Love," Darby R. Slick; Universal Music Publishing Group, BMG Rights Management; performed by Jefferson Airplane.

## Supernatural

Now I am not a film critic or a philosopher, but as I walked home from watching *A Serious Man*, I found myself considering the message of the movie. **I thought about how if God is unknowable and the universe is meaningless then we truly are in a difficult predicament.** I found myself talking to God and seeking to make sense of the movie and my understanding of life. It occurred to me that the Coen brothers start with the presupposition that God does not exist and there is no supernatural power communicating with us. I, on the other hand, was starting from a place of belief in a God who communicates. I was crying out to God to give me some sense that he was there. So I walked and prayed as I made my way along False Creek in Vancouver toward my condo.

As I walked along the seawall of False Creek, a seal popped its head out of the water and began swimming alongside me at the pace of my walk. A second seal raised its head and swam beside it. The two swam along beside me for a while before diving below the surface and disappearing. I had walked along False Creek many times and had never before, and never since, seen seals. I commented to God that it seemed like he had given me a sign to reassure me but that it was so brief that it would be hard to know. As I continued to walk, the two seals appeared and kept pace with me again before diving and disappearing below the surface. I said to God, "If I were a man like Gideon, I might ask for a third time." As if on cue, the two seals appeared beside me a third time, swam beside me for a few more meters, then swam out into the middle of the bay, disappeared below the waves, and did not return. It was one of those moments that left me wondering, "What was that about?" No one I knew had ever had an experience like that along False Creek and seals were not commonly seen there.

I shared this story with a few trusted friends in my faith community. One friend said, "It made me chuckle, because it's not some miraculous display or even a small voice in your head, just this cute little show God put on for you to make you smile and give you a bit of reassurance." Skeptics will say that was all a coincidence—and I cannot say it wasn't. Yet I walked away from that moment amused and reassured. I felt that the Coen brothers were missing something in their understanding of life. Next time seals start following me I'm going to ask God to make the them do tricks! Well, not really. That would be unfair. But it would be fun!

Longing for something more and seeing miracles in the world is something I have spent a lifetime cultivating and I am well-aware of the problem of sharing so many personal experiences in this book. The danger of seeing so many miracles lumped together in one book is that it could seem that I have lived a charmed life and that I have had many prayers miraculously answered. Certainly, I live a life of gratitude for the miracles I have seen, and it is true that I have had a better life than many in this world.

Yet I too have seen long seasons of silence. I have said that I have experienced an average of one or two miracles per decade. The number of times I can be relatively confident that I saw God at work could be counted on my two hands. Much of my life (and most people's lives) has been very ordinary with the usual ups and downs. I too have experienced the late nights with a child whose fever is spiking and have prayed for a quick resolution, only to find that the virus had to take its course. My wife and I have had to work at our marriage and get help from professionals when things were difficult, when we had hoped a simple prayer would provide the solution. There have been many prayers prayed where the answer was *no*. This book is a simple plea to look for, and possibly see, something more than the everyday naturalism that our majority culture shouts into our ears.

## Chapter 13: How *Shall* We Then Live?

In 1976, Francis Schaeffer published a book with a great title: *How Should We Then Live?* In the book he traces history from the time of Rome until 1976 and strongly critiques the influences of the Renaissance, the Enlightenment, and the Rise of Modern Science. He calls people back to living according to the words of the Bible, and specifically the words of Jesus. He claims that this is the only way to have "freedom without chaos."[63] The book was unique because it was historical, theological, academic, accessible, and practical. At points it was controversial and perhaps a little strident in its demands, but it touched at something in Christian circles and had a large following. Schaeffer was able to market the book and a video series based upon the book and called many back to a life of following Jesus. I have intentionally titled this chapter, "How *Shall* We Then Live" to emphasise the point that if there is a supernatural world and a creator God, we will *want* to live a certain way. It is not so much that we *should* or *must* live a certain way, but that we will *desire* to live in a manner that values the words and life of Jesus.

This is an important distinction. I believe it is important to exhibit something that I call, "Humble

---

[63] (Schaeffer 1976)

Apologetics." Let's face it, in recent years, too much of the conversation has been angry. *The New Atheists* such as Richard Dawkins, Sam Harris, Christopher Hitchens, and Stephen Hawking, have come out swinging with angry arguments for why we should not believe in a supernatural God and the Christian Apologists have been all-too-ready to fight back with similar tactics. **We have seen too much debate and not enough conversation; too much enmity and not enough friendship.** Christians have focused too much on proselytizing others to the faith. Can we change the tone?

My friend Robert (who now calls himself an atheist) and I have committed ourselves to being friends despite our deep philosophical divide. We get together for coffee or go to a skeptics' group event; we go together to events like the Bart Campolo/Sean McDowell conversation, or we find some other excuse to get together. We discuss more than our theological and philosophical persuasions. We talk about our kids, our marriages, our friends, and we encourage each other to be good men. I tell him that I don't want to call him an atheist because that is simply anti-something. I call him a humanist. He wants to be a good man, he wants to be a good friend, and he wants to be a good dad. I have told Robert that I am not going to try to convert him from his deconversion; that is between him and God. I tell him that as I remain his friend, I want to see him become the best humanist he can be. He is worried about losing his large network of friends and I encourage people to continue to be his friend. I tell him that I too only see things imperfectly. I see the world just as Paul the Apostle said that he saw the world: dimly, as though he were looking through a bad mirror or an imperfect pane of glass (1 Corinthians 13:12). It keeps me humble to realize I cannot comprehend all that God can see. My words to Robert and to others have become simpler. My simplest questions and his are much the same. I ask my friends to consider with me, "Why is there something rather than nothing?" Do we or our atheist friends have a good answer for that one? "Why are we conscious, for a while (as my friend thinks) or for half an eternity (as I think)?" "How do we live as good humanists or good followers of Jesus?" (as we both wonder).

In 2013, after ten years of planting churches, I found myself in the situation in which many men find themselves when they reach their fifties. I was under-employed with a part-time job at a church and a small business coaching other pastors. I wondered where my career had gone and if I would ever be employed full-time again. My faith in God was at a low, despite the many things I had already seen that drew me to God. My mind was full of doubts about myself, church, and the goodness of God. I was tempted to question whether God existed at all. So, on a warm spring day in April, I told God that I would set down my doubts and fears for three days and spend those days in solitude at a retreat center near the town of Sumas, Washington. During that time, I wrote a journal to keep track of Bible verses I read, and dreams and thoughts I had while at the retreat center. As one might expect on April days in the American Pacific Northwest, it was a rainy time. One afternoon, as a rainstorm had run its course, I went out for a walk. What follows here is my journal entry from the time surrounding that walk.

> I went out for a walk. The rain had stopped for the moment, but it looked like it could start again at any minute. I did not plan to get far from the cabin in case it started pouring again. I went out praying and praising God. I again asked him to show me how I was to earn my daily bread. As I walked around the grounds, I looked up at the top of a little hill called Haystack Hill and could see a cloud or mist hanging around near the top. I felt like God said to me "I am in that cloud. Come on up and we can talk." I hesitated. If I headed for the top of the hill there was a good chance that I would be caught in another rainstorm and get soaked to the skin. God said, "I won't be here long, so you have to hurry. How hard do you want to pursue me? Are you willing to take a chance? Will you show me that you are willing to pursue me hard?" I set out running for the top. It is about a mile of path to the top and much

of it very steep, but I set out running and did not stop running until I was at the top. My lungs were burning, and my heart was pounding but I said to God that I would pursue him as hard as I could, just as I was running this path as hard as I could.

When I got to the top I could not immediately see where the cloud had been. God reassured me that he was still there. He said, "I am here in the blue jay on that branch in front of you. Come a little closer," he seemed to say. I had to go over the top just a few feet and past some trees to the bench that sits on the edge of the lookout. Then I could see the cloud that I had chased. I sat on the bench and for a brief moment the cloud came up the hill just a bit and enveloped the bench on which I sat. Then it receded back to the spot just below the top of the hill and the blue jay flew into the midst of it. The Spirit said to me, "I am here in the cloud and in the jay." The wind was blowing all around my ears and blowing all the clouds away from the top of the hill, but this one cloud was protected in the shelter of the hilltop and stayed right where it was.

God urged me to take off my shoes. I was standing on holy ground. I felt foolish. I said, "God are you sure? If I take off my shoes and socks I will get my feet all dirty and then when I go back down my socks and shoes will get dirty on the inside." He asked if I was willing to listen to him. I said yes and took off my shoes and socks and stood barefoot on a wet, muddy, cold path strewn with pine needles and sharp rocks. I asked God what message he had for me. He said, **"This is real. These impressions you have been hearing are from me. You are learning how to hear the Spirit of the Lord. You can trust what you hear."** I stood there praying for a while, asking God to confirm the things he had been saying to me already. He said that I could trust them as much as any man can trust these sensations. I told him I wanted to breathe the air of heaven, but my lungs were not yet equipped for that. I wanted to hear from him, but my ears were not well-tuned to him. He told me it is enough that I am listening and that I should go out and look for confirmations of the things I had been hearing.

The cloud began to fade but still the blue jay stayed right there on the branch just a little below me on the hill. I prayed that God would not leave yet. He said he would never leave me or forsake me but that this sign was just about over. The cloud thinned to nothing and the jay suddenly dove off the tree branch down into the foliage lower on the hill to a place where I could no longer see it.

I walked back to the bench to get my shoes and socks. My feet were still warm and only now did I realize that the path was sharp on the soles of my feet. I began to wonder if I was going crazy. Was this some sort of schizophrenic break from reality? The impressions I heard in my mind were, "You are no crazier than Moses, no crazier than Noah, no crazier than Abraham, no crazier than Peter, no crazier than Paul. You have had an encounter with God. He has brought reassurance. You have a new thin place[64]

---

[64] The concept of a "thin place" is a metaphor for a place in which the distance between heaven and earth is thin, allowing greater connectivity between a person and God. For further explanation see Mark D. Roberts treatment of the topic at

in which God has met you." I thought back to a couple of years previously when I had stayed at this same retreat center and cried out to God. I had tried hard to hear from God but had not heard anything. I had climbed up to this same hilltop and had begged for a message from God, but I had heard nothing but the wind. This time I had approached God with a better frame of mind. I prepared myself by spending much time in the Bible; I prayed for myself but also for others. I told God that I would take anything from his hand whether it was for me or for someone else. I rested in him and wrote about my impressions in an electronic journal.

As I slowly walked down the hill, I spoke to God some more. I thanked him for his creation. I spoke of how much easier it is to see his handiwork out here in the woods than in the city. The city covers up the raw energy of streams running through the forest. The towering trees that are grown over with moss remind me of life that is older than me, the sound

---

https://www.patheos.com/blogs/markdroberts/series/thin-places/

of the birds, the smells of the soil, the taste of the stream, all speak of the grandeur of God. They proclaim that he is here, and he is not silent. I was struck with how hard it is to believe that all of the universe just came into being. I thought about how if there were no God, "Why would there be something rather than nothing?" I know that some of my atheist friends would say that the universe might have always been. It might just as easily be eternal as an eternal God. But I spoke to God of how **God seems to be just the sort of thing that you would expect to be eternal. Universes do not seem like the sort of thing that would be eternal.**

On my way back past the upper pond on the property I saw a beautiful turtle about the size of a laptop sitting on a log that was half-submerged along the shore of the pond. The turtle was sitting there catching the warmth of the sun as it had poked out from the clouds. He looked totally content with the God who watches over him and every other living creature on the planet. He stretched his neck and raised his head toward the sun; or was it toward God in a gesture of praise? As I made my way back to the place where I had first seen the cloud on the hill top it was obvious that it was completely gone. The phenomenon had been brief and I had managed to get to the top of the hill before it disappeared.

Some will say that the whole event was a product of an overactive imagination and I would be hard-pressed to prove them wrong. Yet the experience has gained more significance over the last six years as I have watched my career progress with what I believe to be the help of God. Within three months of the experience I had a full-time job with a church I had always respected. My role with this church has changed many times but continues to this day and has been a great source of professional development and a source of spiritual growth for me and for those I have served in this capacity. As with many previous presumed miracles, the fruit of the experience has been abundant. It has changed the way I live and allowed me to more fully live by faith.

So where does this leave us? This book is of course written from my perspective with as much objectivity as I can give it while seeking to have a humble opinion of my detachment from the emotions of the experiences. All of us must admit to our own bias and the lens through which we see the world. I hope that you have caught my heart, my humble apologetics, and my willingness to admit that I am not free of bias. I hope that the reader can also see that they too have bias and a lens that colors the way they see the world. I hope too that in writing this book I may at least inspire us all to approach life with a little more reverence. **There is mystery and uncertainty in this life, and it should be approached with amazement, humility, and gratitude as we consider how many things we really don't know.** Perhaps we need to remember to tremble. Nichole Nordeman, in a song written by Albert Collins, suggests a posture of reverence to the God of the universe when she sings:

> Oh let me not forget to tremble
> Face down on the ground do I dare to
> take the liberty to stare at you
> Oh let me not forget to tremble[65]

Nordeman is reminding us of how easy it is for me to walk boldly into the presence of God without any thought of who he is. I would never enter the throne room of Queen Elizabeth in such a cavalier manner. Why do I feel it is acceptable to do so with the God of the universe? May I never forget to tremble.

Annie Dillard puts it this way:

---

[65] "Tremble," Albert Collins, © Universal Music Publishing Group. This brief portion of the lyrics has been quoted for intellectual purposes, full lyrics can be found here: https://bit.ly/2VjlbxY.

Now we are no longer primitive. Now the whole world seems not holy.... We as a people have moved from pantheism to pan-atheism.... It is difficult to undo our own damage and to recall to our presence that which we have asked to leave. It is hard to desecrate a grove and change your mind. We doused the burning bush and cannot rekindle it. We are lighting matches in vain under every green tree. Did the wind used to cry and the hills shout forth praise? Now speech has perished from among the lifeless things of the earth, and living things say very little to very few.... And yet it could be that wherever there is motion there is noise, as when a whale breaches and smacks the water, and wherever there is stillness there is the small, still voice, God's speaking from the whirlwind, nature's old song and dance, the show we drove from town.... What have we been doing all these centuries but trying to call God back to the mountain, or, failing that, raise a peep out of anything that isn't us? What is the difference between

a cathedral and a physics lab? Are they
not both saying: Hello?[66]

Some of us let go of the idea of the supernatural so long ago that we will find it hard to see faint impressions of the holy in the world around us. We might search without finding because we do not see.

Okay, here is where we take a deep breath and consider. There are a number of ways to proceed from here. The following list features some of the options open to all of us but I will address them to the reader.
1. You might actually be convinced that God exists and that it is time to give him a try.
2. You may have been aware of God a long time ago but have not seen supernatural answers to prayer and now want to look for some.
3. You may believe in God but may not know how to reach the creator of the universe. What religion or method allows one to communicate with this God? Go ahead, do some research. See which approaches to life and religion make the most sense. I am convinced that God's truth will shine through.
4. You may still be on the fence about God and still have questions about the nature of God. Don't shove those feelings under the carpet. Keep

---

[66] Annie Dillard in *Teaching a Stone to Talk* as Quoted by Francis Collins in *The Language of God*.

wrestling with your ambivalence.
5. You may still feel there is not enough evidence to believe in God. Look for more.

**This book will not answer all of the questions. It has a very narrow purpose: to open minds to the possibility of the supernatural.** I want to be available to explore such things with you further. You can reach me at my blog site by searching the name "Keith Shields." If this book has convinced you to give God a try, I encourage you to take slow steps toward him. C.S. Lewis recounts (in *Mere Christianity*) that he went from atheist to deist to Christian over a period of time. Perhaps you will need some more time. Make a start today and keep pursuing God wherever the pursuit takes you.

On the other hand, maybe this book has moved you to want to participate in seeing the supernatural break into this world. Perhaps you would like to increase your prayer effectiveness and would like to see God work in supernatural ways in your life and in the lives of others. If you are ready for prayer, how will the reasoning of this book affect your prayer life? Early on in my prayer journey, I learned to pray from an unlikely source. I say unlikely considering that I was a farm boy from Central Alberta and one would normally not expect a South Korean pastor to be a likely mentor. Yet a small book by Dr. David Yonggi Cho from South Korea had a profound effect on me in my early prayer life. In *The Fourth*

*Dimension*,[67] Cho suggests the following prayer process. He tells us to:
1. Pray specifically – envision a clear-cut objective,
2. Have a burning desire – Psalm 37:4 says that he will give you the desires of your heart,
3. Pray for assurance – until you sense that you have the answer, and
4. Speak the word – proclaim the answer to your prayer.

I have made this type of prayer my more or less constant companion for over 30 years with varying degrees of confidence and I would encourage others to try it as well. You may also want to read the book; the details are in the bibliographic notes at the end of this work.

Perhaps this present book, *Supernatural*, has only muddied the waters for you; perhaps you are still not convinced that God and a supernatural world exist. Perhaps you are sitting on the fence or you are with Bart Campolo and cannot see any evidence for a supernatural world. If either is the case, I encourage you to contact me so we can talk about your perspective. Maybe you would like to convince me of your outlook. **You have listened to me for the length of this book; I would be glad to listen to you.** My friend Robert is trying to evangelise me to become an atheist (even though I have told him that I will not try to re-evangelise him to the Christian faith) and

---

[67] (Cho 1979, 1-21)

Bart Campolo is an evangelist for his brand of humanism as he travels North America. I welcome the conversation.

But here is my parting comment to those of you who are still on the fence and those who have given up on a supernatural perspective. What if just one of the supernatural events suggested in this book is real? What if God *does* exist? Would he not try to communicate with you in some way? Is he not worth investigating to see what kind of God he is? Open yourself to the possibility and see where it leads. I highly recommend the life of faith.

## Works Cited

Adomnan, and Richard Sharpe (Translator). 1991. *Life of St. Columba.* New York: Penguin Books.

Augustine. 426. *de Civitate Dei (City of God).*

Brueggemann, Walter. 1997. *Cadences of Home.* Louisville: Westminster John Knox Press.

Cahill, Thomas. 1996. *How the Irish Saved Civilization.* New York: Anchor Books.

Cho, David Yonggi. 1979. *The Fourth Dimension: Discovering a new world of answered prayer.* Newberry: Bridge Logos.

DeCenso, Frank Jr. (ed.). 2009. *Amazed by the Power of God.* Shippensburg: Destiny Image.

*Denver Post.* 2013. "Vatican: Healing of Colorado Springs boy a miracle." April 13: https://www.denverpost.com/2013/04/13/vatican-healing-of-colorado-springs-boy-a-miracle/.

Draper, Electa . 2016. "Vatican declares healing of Colorado Springs boy a miracle after prayers to German nun." *Denver Post*, April 30.

Fee, Gordon D. 2006. *The Disease of the Prosperity Gospels.* Vancouver: Regent College Publishing.

2012. "Holy Bible New Living Translation." Carol Stream: Tyndale House Publishers, Inc.

Keener, Craig S. 2011. *Miracles: The Credibility of the New Testament Accounts, 2 Volumes.* Baker Academic.

Lamott, Anne. 2017. *TED: Ideas Worth Spreading.* April. Accessed June 30, 2019. https://www.ted.com/talks/anne_lamott_12_truths_i_learned_from_life_and_writing?language=en.

Lewis, C.S. 2015. *Mere Christianity.* San Francisco: HarperSanFrancisco.

—. 2015. *Miracles.* HarperOne.

—. 1950. *The Lion, the Witch, and the Wardrobe.* Samuel French Ltd.

—. 1980. *The Screwtape Letters: How a senior devil instructs a junior devil in the art of temptation.* New York: MacMillan Publishing Co., Inc.

McKnight, Scot. 2019. "Recent Stories of Leaving the Faith." *Jesus Creed.* August 20. Accessed August 23, 2019. https://www.patheos.com/blogs/jesuscreed/2019/08/20/recent-stories-of-leaving-the-faith/?utm_medium=webpush&utm_source=evangelical&utm_campaign=JesusCreed.

MDM. 2016. *Vancouver As It Was.* May 26. Accessed June 26, 2019.

https://vanasitwas.wordpress.com/2016/05/20/charles-s-price-healing-in-vancouver/.

Peers, E. Allison, and Teresa. 2007. *The Interior Castle*. Dover Publications.

Price, Charles S. 2017. *The Story of My Life (1887-1947)*. Jawbone Digital.

Romez, Clarissa, David Zaritzky, and Joshua W. Brown. 2019. "Case Report of gastroparesis healing: 16 years of a chronic syndrome resolved after proximal intercessory prayer." *Complementary Therapies in Medicine* 43: 289-294.

Schaeffer, Francis. 1976. *How Should We Then Live?: The Rise and Fall of Western Thought and Culture*. Grand Rapids: Fleming H Revell Co.

Stafford, Tim. 2012. *Miracles*. Bloomington: Bethany House Publishers.

Wikipedia. 2018. ""Scotland in the Early Middle Ages"." *Wikipedia*. Accessed 11 17, 2018. https://en.wikipedia.org/wiki/Scotland_in_the_Early_Middle_Ages.

Yordan, Edgardo. 2017. "How the Catholic Church Validates Medical Miracles." February 11. Accessed 05 31, 2019. https://www.youtube.com/watch?v=LqoKvkH5Val.

www.ingramcontent.com/pod-product-compliance
Lightning Source LLC
Chambersburg PA
CBHW030327100526
44592CB00010B/602